Also read Fr. Mackin's

A Spirituality for Sunday People (Year B) and
Integrity: Living God's Word (Year C)

ENJOYING GOD'S
GIFTS

FR. KEVIN E. MACKIN, OFM

WESTBOW
PRESS®
A DIVISION OF THOMAS NELSON
& ZONDERVAN

WestBow Press books may be ordered through booksellers or by contacting:

WestBow Press
A Division of Thomas Nelson & Zondervan
1663 Liberty Drive
Bloomington, IN 47403
www.westbowpress.com
1 (866) 928-1240

ISBN: 978-1-9736-3959-6 (sc)
ISBN: 978-1-9736-3961-9 (hc)
ISBN: 978-1-9736-3960-2 (e)

Library of Congress Control Number: 2018910815

Print information available on the last page.

WestBow Press rev. date: 09/28/2018

Dedicated to the parishioners of St. Raphael Church
in St. Petersburg, Florida.

They are gifts of God, bringing joy to the world.

CONTENTS

INTRODUCTION

I am happy to present *Enjoying God's Gifts*, year A in a three-volume series reflecting on the Sunday lectionary Bible readings. (Year B is titled *A Spirituality for Sunday People*, and year C is *Integrity: Living God's Word*.)

We may wonder whether God speaks to us. He does, especially through the inspired word of God, the Bible. This is a privileged form of conversation between God and us.

Wherever you are in the spiritual life, God has something to say to you.

With every reading, new understandings of our life with God will emerge, and we will be better inspired to enjoy God's many gifts for us. God speaks to us in the Bible so we can grow in holiness. Holiness is all about growing more and more in the likeness of God. It's a continuing process.

God authored the Bible in the sense that the Bible includes what God wants us to know about God, ourselves, and the universe. But the human authors of the Bible were real authors. They employed the languages, images, literary genres, and worldviews they knew to communicate basic religious truths, not scientific truths.

Moreover, the Bible isn't one book but a library. We can find prose and poetry, fiction and history, myths and legends, historical narratives and short stories, genealogies and sermons, parables and letters, songs and rules, prophetic and proverbial sayings, and apocalyptic visions.

Some texts in the Bible evolved over decades; others came over centuries. In fact, at least forty authors probably wrote the Bible over fifteen hundred years. These books aren't always easily understandable.

The most frequent exposure to the word of God is through the Catholic lectionary, from which lectors and presiders read specific biblical passages for each liturgy. The lectionary contains the heart of the Bible, most of the Old and New Testaments, and the book of the Gospels, from which the Sunday gospel is proclaimed. This collection comprises the liturgical Bible.

Each of the four Gospels notes explicitly that the resurrection took place on the first day of the week, the day we call Sunday. That's why Christians from the earliest times gathered to celebrate the resurrection. In changing times, amid "bad news," the celebration helps to keep our faith in the "good news" alive, the understanding that we are destined for eternal life within the life of the triune God.

In the course of time, the weeks of the year were organized into two "seasons": Advent and Christmas, and Lent and Easter. Between those seasons we have two periods of "ordinary time," so named for the Latin *ordo*, "order of things."

Usually we start reading a book at the beginning and proceed to the end. There are also some books—treasured books—from which we select a familiar passage that's appropriate at a particular time. During the liturgical year, we read the Bible in each of these two ways.

In ordinary time, we read from the Gospels of Matthew (in year A), Mark (year B), and Luke (year C). We also read selections from other books of the Bible. The first reading is followed by a selection from the book of Psalms.

For the seasons of Advent and Christmas, and Lent and Easter, we read in light of a theme. God's wonderful plan for us is revealed in the birth, life, death, and resurrection of Jesus. The Gospel according to John is especially featured.

The early Christians also celebrated the actual day of the Lord's resurrection. We enter Easter by our baptism. That's why we say, "In baptism I died with Christ and now share in his risen life." In the fourth and fifth centuries, the church developed a system of rites to accompany the faith journey of those elected to be baptized at Easter. Baptism is the key to understanding the Lenten scripture selections. Lent is a forty-day retreat before baptism.

The Bible ultimately is about Jesus. The apostle Paul informed us that the sacred scriptures are "capable of giving you wisdom for salvation through faith in Christ Jesus." (2 Tm 3:15) And Paul spoke to a society not unlike our own. But the followers of Christ are called to be different. "Remain faithful," Paul wrote, "to what you have learned and believed" (2 Tm 3:14).

The key to understanding the meaning of the liturgical year lies in the notion of "presence." We believe the living Christ is truly present in the Eucharist under the appearance of bread and wine and that the living Christ is present in his word, since he himself speaks when the scriptures are read. And the living Christ is present in a special, mysterious way when we celebrate the various moments in the liturgical year, the history of our salvation.

God's wonderful plan for us is revealed in the birth, life, death, and resurrection of Jesus. After four weeks of Advent expectation, we celebrate at Christmas not only Christ's birth in Bethlehem but also his birth in us. We celebrate our discipleship and baptismal call to bring Christ to birth in our own time, place, and culture.

As we celebrate the mysteries of the living Christ during the year, we believe we enter God's "time of salvation" (2 Cor 6:2) so that we, through grace and mystery, become present to that particular moment. Yes, we enter the stages of Jesus's life and his mysteries through word and sacrament.

In celebrating this annual liturgical cycle of Christ's mysteries, the church honors Mary, the Mother of God. Mary bore Jesus in her womb and gave him birth. Today we bear Christ within ourselves, and we pray to bring forth Christ in our world by word and example.

In addition, the liturgical year celebrates the lives of holy men and women from every continent and century. When we recall the saints, the focus is on what God has accomplished in them, and we are led to contemplate what God wants to accomplish in us.

St. Paul described all scripture as "inspired by God" (2 Tm 3:16), inspired not simply as artists, poets, composers, and musicians are. The Bible actually has God's breath, his Spirit. Through the Bible, God speaks to us.

I hope you enjoy reading the series of books based on my Sunday homilies ... drama, humor, and all. I pray they will help you encounter the living Christ in the Bible and the word proclaimed Sunday after Sunday—and that you will enjoy the fullness of God's many gifts.

Our global Catholic Church is a biblical community of disciples in the sense that it acknowledges and proclaims the Bible as the word of God in human form. In particular, the scriptures point to Jesus as the unique, definitive revelation of God to us. In other words, everything God ever wanted to do or say to us he did and said in Jesus. The church as a community of disciples is the instrument of the Spirit, who guides us along the journey to eternal life in the light of new questions in new generations and new problems in new cultures.

Every author owes an indebtedness to certain people, especially for their attention to detail. I am particularly indebted to Janet Gianopoulos, whose invaluable assistance lightened the challenge of publishing this series. A deep and lasting sense of gratitude goes to her.

FIRST SUNDAY OF ADVENT

Over the holidays, I came across a much-beloved pastor emeritus in the Diocese of St. Petersburg. He shared an edifying perspective I want to pass along. After I greeted him warmly with a "How are you doing?" he responded, "I'm well, thanks. But the house in which I live is dilapidated. It's beginning to totter on its foundations. Its roof is terribly worn. Its walls shake with every wind. This old house is almost uninhabitable, and I think that soon I will have to move out of it. But I'm doing quite well, thank you."

I appreciate his image. The body is beginning to break down, but he himself is doing well. I empathize with that; do you? Advent reminds us that one day we will have to "move out," but happily we have another home to move into, our heavenly dwelling place.

Especially during the Advent and Christmas season, many people seem to be searching for the secret to happiness.

Someone wrote that all it takes to be happy is to do the following: forgive, apologize (we all make mistakes), listen to advice, check your temper, share the blame, make the best out of situations (most things seldom work out perfectly), and put the needs of others before your own.

Let's practice as many of these secrets to happiness as we can during this holiday season. We'll soon have a more positive outlook on life. That's what Advent is all about, hope in the future—a glorious future. So we pray during the Advent season, "Come, Lord Jesus, and transfigure us into new creatures; recreate this universe of ours into a 'new heaven and new earth.'" "Come, Lord Jesus" is the so-called "maranatha prayer" in the last chapter of the book of Revelation.

As we reflect on global, political, and environmental challenges (for example, the war in Syria, threats to peace from Russia and North Korea, random acts of terrorism in Iraq and Afghanistan, and recent floods and famines), we may recall the sentiments of William Butler Yeats, who wrote the following in his great poem "The Second Coming":

> Things fall apart; the center cannot hold; mere anarchy
> is loosed upon the world, the blood dimm'd tide is loosed,
> the best lack all convictions, while the worst are full of
> passionate intensity.

But Advent speaks loudly and clearly against those sentiments Yeats captured. Advent invites us to reflect on the threefold coming of Jesus. Yes, Jesus came to us centuries ago in Bethlehem of Judea. He comes to us now sacramentally in the liturgy, and he will come again in great power and glory at the end-time.

So how might we celebrate Advent? Some families create a wreath with four candles and then light one candle at the dinner table during the first week, two candles during the second week, and so on. Upon lighting the candle, they pray in their own words for the coming anew of the Messiah in their lives. Other families make a Jesse or genealogy tree to recapture the story of our salvation as told in the Hebrew Bible. Still others set up a nativity scene and invite family members to take turns telling in their own words the meaning of Christmas or "God with us," Emmanuel. These are but a few customs that can help us keep the meaning of Advent alive.

The word of God in today's liturgy describes the eighth century before Jesus (the 700s). The Assyrian armies had overrun northern Israel. Despite this catastrophe, the prophet Isaiah spoke about hope, a major theme of Advent (Isa 2:1–5).

Some philosophers argue that hope is a fundamental characteristic of human existence. In fact, some of you may be hoping that I will give a very brief homily.

In any case, the prophet proclaimed that people everywhere "shall go up" to the temple in Jerusalem—which symbolizes God's presence—not only to hear the word of God but also to do the word. And everywhere there will be peace. Yes, nations will transform weapons of war into instruments of peace. People will seek to do the right thing.

As we reflect on our future, we might ask whether we always hope in God, especially when what is happening to us is the opposite of what we want. And yes, do we always try to do what is right?

In his letter to the Christian community at Rome, Paul spoke about his life and ours drawing closer to the end every day—whether that be the day of Christ's glorious return or the day of our individual entry into eternity. Stay awake, be ready, live in the light, advised St. Paul. Practice virtue. Care for one another, pray earnestly, please God in your everyday behavior, and always be ready to meet Jesus (Rom 13:11–14).

In the Gospel according to Matthew, Jesus spoke to us about watchfulness or readiness. Jesus may come to us suddenly when we least expect him. And so, live each day as though it were your last (Mt 24:37–44).

I close, noting Thornton Wilder's classic play *Our Town*. In one scene in a small, early twentieth-century town, a father says quietly to his teenage son something like this: "I saw your mother chopping wood. She gets up early, cooks, washes – and still she has to go out and chop wood. I suppose she got tired of asking you. And you eat her meals and put on the clothes she keeps nice for you – but she's not your servant, she's your mother -- and you run off and play baseball." The teen begins to get a bit teary-eyed with remorse, and his father lovingly brings the moment to an end, saying, "Well, I knew all I had to do was call your attention to it."

We take so much for granted, don't we? We sometimes take one another for granted without even a thank-you. We take God and his gifts to us for granted. We take our freedoms and opportunities for granted without even a word of gratitude. We take tomorrow for granted without a second thought.

Today's word of God says loudly and clearly, "Don't take tomorrow for granted." Like the scene in *Our Town*, it's easy to imagine God saying to each of us something like, "I looked and saw something I didn't like to see. I've seen it many times. I saw your sisters and brothers in need of you. Some went without what they needed because of you." And Jesus adds ever so gently, "I knew I'd only have to mention it to you."

The great truth of our faith is that we are by grace what Jesus Christ is by nature—sons and daughters of God our Father, called to live lives worthy of that dignity.

This Advent season, may we help the Lord bring peace to those who are troubled, faith to those who doubt, hope to those who despair, courage to those who are weak, healing to those who are sick, joy to those who are sad, a compass to those who are lost, and life everlasting to those who have died.

SECOND SUNDAY OF ADVENT

I heard a story about two ninety-year-old men, Mike and Pat. They played minor league baseball together. They were the best of friends. When Mike was terminally ill, Pat saw him every day. Pat finally asked Mike to do him a favor. "When you get to heaven, Mike, let me know if there's baseball in heaven."

Mike looked up from his deathbed and said, "Pat, if I can, I will." And shortly after that, Mike died.

A few nights later, a flash of light woke Pat, and a voice whispered, "Pat, it's Mike. I'm in heaven, and I've got some very good news and a little bad news."

Pat said, "Tell me the good news first."

The voice whispered, "The good news is that there is baseball in heaven. Our buddies are here, we're young again, it's always springtime, and we can play baseball all we want."

Pat said, "That's fantastic. So, what's the bad news?"

"You'll be pitching up here next Tuesday." Life is full of surprises.

How many of you have begun Christmas shopping? We may be spending more time than we should in search of that perfect gift.

During Advent, I invite you to treasure the gifts or gems you already have in your own house: family and friends, colleagues and neighbors.

I often think of what Marian Wright Edelman, a children's advocate, wrote in her autobiography. "I no longer remember most of the presents I found under the tree as a child. But I carry with me and treasure the lessons in life my parents and good neighbors taught me throughout my childhood."

Her point is simple: some gifts can really transform the lives of people we love, such as gifts of teaching; listening and supporting; sharing time and experiences; and compassion, forgiveness, and affirmation.

This kind of giving begins in our families and reaches out to our workplaces and communities. I hope all of us will think of these enduring gifts we can give to one another this season.

The word of God takes us back to a prophet in ancient Israel by the name of Isaiah. Isaiah here spoke about an ideal king who possessed wisdom and intelligence, courage and empathy, good judgment, and wonder and awe at our great God (Isa 11:1–10). Would that politicians everywhere manifested these gifts.

This ideal king, Isaiah said, will usher in a kingdom of peace, justice, truth, and freedom.

Isaiah's words might ask us how we exemplify these baptismal gifts in our everyday lives. These gifts include wisdom (to recognize what truly matters), intelligence (to see what's true), courage (to stand up for what's right), empathy (to care for the needy), good judgment (to do the right thing for the greater common good), and wonder and awe (to worship the great God of this universe).

In his letter to the Christian community in Rome, Paul called for reconciliation among the different factions in that community. He asked them to accept, love, and support one another as Jesus unconditionally accepted, loved, and forgave them (Rom 15:4–9). Why? So they could live and work together to make their community even better.

Paul's words may be asking us to practice virtue, the key organizing principle of a good society. But what is virtue? It's a habitual and firm disposition to do good. Virtue leads to better people, better living, better relationships, and a better world.

In the Gospel according to Matthew, John the Baptizer appeared in the wilderness with a message of immediacy. He proclaimed repentance, a turning away from self-centeredness to an others-centered, God-centered life. The Messiah, John said, was about to come (Mt 3:1–12).

John the Baptizer's words challenge us to examine our own consciences. Do we live God-centered lives?

Now, the Advent season is about waiting. We do plenty of waiting, don't we? We wait in line at Lowe's or Home Depot. Luckily there's online shopping. We wait in a doctor's office. We wait at the airport. Yes, we do a lot of waiting. And so too did the ancient Hebrews, as Isaiah reminded us. But theirs was a different kind of waiting. They often waited for the Messiah to rescue them—yes, from their hardships in ancient Egypt, from the follies of their kings, from their exile in Babylonia, and from their sufferings throughout their many foreign occupations.

And yet the Messiah often didn't seem to "rescue" them. In fact, he often appeared to be hidden from them.

In many ways, we are like the Hebrews. We often pray to God to rescue us from a crisis of one kind or another—for example, a severe illness, a job loss, a broken friendship, or a divorce. We beg God to suddenly appear and make things right. In fact, some would say this is the story of everyone. Think, for example, of the people who have lost loved ones in wars, addictions, or accidents. They may ask, Where was God? Why didn't God protect their loved ones? Why didn't God make sure they weren't in the wrong place at the wrong time? There are, of course, really no satisfactory answers.

Yes, we often pray for God to rescue us from this or that or to make this or that right. And yet God seems silent, hidden.

But is God silent? Is God hidden?

We profess that God is in our midst, not in a manger. That event happened centuries ago in Bethlehem.

Where is God? All around us. In nature, in sunrises and sunsets. God is in us, deep within our own selves. Why? Because we are a community of faith, and wherever two or three gather in Jesus's name, there God is. He is in the Word proclaimed; He is in the signs of bread and wine. He is at the core of our being.

We cannot touch the God-man Jesus like the first disciples did. We can't sit at his feet, break bread with him, or stand near him crucified as they did. And yet he is here—in all of us gathered together in faith.

And what does all this mean—God with us, Emmanuel? St. Paul wrote centuries ago that God's favor, grace, and eternal life have been revealed to us in Jesus. This is the good news, the gospel. And this Jesus, once crucified and now risen, anticipates what we hope to become. And until he comes, we should continue the saving work of Jesus Christ.

Let us pray during this Advent season that the Spirit of God who dwells within us will empower us anew to become better instruments of faith in God, hope in eternal life, and love of one another. May we be channels of forgiveness, compassion, truth, and fairness; as well as instruments of hospitality, service, and responsibility. Then we will reexperience a change of heart, a change of attitudes and behaviors John the Baptizer called for so the risen Christ will recognize us as his disciples when he does come to us in the mystery of our own dying.

THIRD SUNDAY OF ADVENT

The third Sunday of Advent is known as Gaudete Sunday. The word *Gaudete* is a Latin verb that translates into English as "rejoice." We should rejoice because Jesus, the joy of our salvation, is about to be born.

I read about a youngster who asked his mother, "Where do people come from?" The mother thought for a minute and replied, "Well, Joey, God made Adam and Eve, and they had children, and that's where we came from." Two days later, the youngster asked his father the same question. The reply? "The human race evolved from apes over millions of years." The confused youngster went back to his mother and said, "Mommy, you told me that God created people, but Daddy says they came from apes." "Well, Joey, it's very simple. I told you about my side of the family, and Daddy told you about his." There's something not quite right about that answer.

Here's a question. How many can sing "The Twelve Days of Christmas"?

There's a story behind that carol. After 1558, for some two centuries thereafter, Catholics in England couldn't practice their faith openly. And so someone wrote "The Twelve Days of Christmas" as a statement about Catholic belief. The carol has two levels of meaning.

On a religious level, the partridge in a pear tree is Jesus Christ. The two turtle doves are the Old and New Testaments. Three French hens are faith, hope, and love. Four calling birds are the four Gospels. The five golden rings refer to the Torah. Six geese a-laying stand for the six days of creation. Seven swans a-swimming are the seven gifts of the Spirit. Eight maids a-milking are the eight beatitudes. Nine ladies dancing are the fruit of the Spirit. The ten lords a-leaping are the Ten Commandments. Eleven pipers piping stand for the faithful disciples. And the twelve drummers drumming symbolize the twelve points of belief in the Apostles' Creed.

So if you listen to or sing "The Twelve Days of Christmas" this season, you might test your family's religious education.

The word of God takes us back, probably to the Isaiah of the sixth century before Jesus. Babylonia had conquered Jerusalem, burned the temple down, and destroyed whatever it could. Yet the author spoke about new beginnings. The desert "will rejoice and bloom," the wilderness will "burst forth" with waters and streams, the blond will see, the deaf will hear, the lame "shall leap like a stag." (Isa 35:1–6, 10).

The words of the author of Isaiah may be asking us, What message do we proclaim to others in our attitudes and behaviors? Hope in a God-centered future? The medium is the message.

In his letter James urged us to practice patience like the farmer, he said, who plants and waits for nature to bring forth a harvest of produce. Have patience. Even better, have perseverance. That's a theme in James (Jas 5:7–10).

History abounds with examples of naysayers. However, success often comes to those who persevere, who say, "I can make it happen."

A sculptor, for example, worked on a large piece of marble and lamented, "I can't do anything with it." But Michelangelo discovered the same stone and visualized the possibilities for it. His I-can-make-it-happen attitude resulted in one of the greatest masterpieces in sculpture, the statue of David.

Thomas Edison discouraged his friend Henry Ford from pursuing the idea of a motorcar. But Ford believed he could make it happen. And of course he did. Yes, patience and perseverance often make the difference. James's words might well be asking us, How persevering are we in our lives of discipleship with Jesus?

In the Gospel of Matthew, John the Baptizer announced that he was the voice in the wilderness who prepared the way for the Messiah. John cried out to the people who came to the waters of the Jordan, "Repent" and live an others-centered, God-centered life. And when Jesus walked along the banks of the Jordan, John pointed to him as the sacrificial Lamb of God, through whose bloody death and glorious resurrection we are in relationship with God (Mt 11:2–11).

What really caught my attention today were the words of Isaiah— "Fear not"—and the courage of John the Baptizer. John had the courage to speak truth to power—King Herod—and paid for it with his life. He wasn't afraid to do the right thing. He is a profile in courage.

It's interesting that a common phrase in the New Testament is "Do not be afraid." A common phrase in the Old Testament is "Be not afraid." Between the two testaments, the phrases appear more than one thousand times. Do you think God may be trying to get a message across to us?

Some psychologists argue that the most dominant emotion in society is fear. Think about it. We're afraid of rejection and failure, certain parts of town, certain types of people, criticism—and afraid to say how we really feel and what we really think. We're afraid of so many things. All these fears can paralyze us. In fact, fear stops more people from doing something extraordinary than lack of ability.

Courage isn't the absence of fear but the acquired ability to move beyond it.

Look through the pages of history and identify people you admire. Who would they have been without courage? I would venture to say that nothing worthwhile in life is achieved without courage. So much can be accomplished in one moment of courage. By the same token, so much can be lost in one moment of fear.

Courage is an acquired virtue. You learn to ride a bicycle by riding a bicycle. You learn to play a sport or a musical instrument by playing. You acquire courage by practicing courage.

Virtues are like muscles—when you exercise them, they become stronger. John Glenn, for example, logged thousands of aeronautical miles before he became the first American to orbit the earth.

Starting a new venture, making a sacramental commitment such as marriage or ordination, struggling to overcome an addiction, coming humbly before God in prayer—they all require courage. Courage animates us and makes so many things possible. In fact, the measure of one's life is the measure of one's courage.

It takes courage to do something just right, as Therese of Lisieux did daily when called on to choose between quality and what's slipshod or just enough.

It takes courage to stand on principle and an informed conscience, as Thomas More did against Henry VIII, when More was called on to speak up for what was right.

In short, it takes courage to choose what is right in decisions that affect work, career, family, and social life. We know that in the struggles of life, we are not alone, for God has given us the spirit of courage.

Yes, the challenges of leading a good life demand courage. In the end, a life lived in accordance with an informed conscience leaves us at peace within ourselves. And only such a life—and the struggle to have an informed conscience—can bestow this peace, this inner calm that comes from being in harmony not only with God but also with our own inner best selves.

And so, seek always what is right as John the Baptizer did—not what is fashionable, what is expected by others, or what is merely acceptable but simply what is right and good.

Fourth Sunday of Advent

During the Christmas holidays, I'm forgetting the many challenges the media says we will face in the next four years. After all, our ancestors faced similar challenges. For example, Cicero, a Roman statesman and author, wrote in 55 BC, "The … budget must be balanced." Cicero would be shocked by today's national debt.

Socrates, a fifth-century BC Athenian philosopher, attacked earlier generations for destroying the forests and landscape. Yes, Socrates would probably join today's global warming movement.

And Livy, a Roman historian in the first century AD, objected to the moral rot and slipping standards of conduct in society. So maybe it really is true: there's nothing new under the sun.

This is indeed a festive time of year. Children are excited about the arrival of Santa Claus, houses flash with lights, stores are jammed with shoppers, and online circuits are overloaded.

Amid this excitement, we can easily forget the true meaning of Christmas.

Symbols—a tree, candle, ornament, or angel—can invite us to reflect on the true meaning of Christmas and bow down like the shepherds or wise men to worship the Christ child.

Three biblical personalities dominate the Advent season: Isaiah, who prophesized a Messiah; John the Baptist, who prepared the way for the Messiah; and the Virgin Mary, who gave birth to the Messiah, the Christ child. In today's gospel a fourth personality appears, Joseph.

In today's word of God, the author of Isaiah realized that the Hebrew

King Ahaz was in a quandary. Mighty Assyria threatened his kingdom. Should he join an anti-Assyrian alliance? Or trust in God? What should he do?

Isaiah begged the king, "Ask for a sign from God" so he would know what to do. But the king refused.

And so Isaiah prophesized that God himself would give a sign. A young woman would bear a child, Emmanuel or "God with us." Isaiah's point is simple: God never reneges on his promises, even when others do. David's dynasty will continue forever (Isa 7:10–14).

Later, early Christianity saw the prophecy fulfilled in the birth of Jesus, whose name means "He will save." Jesus is indeed our way, our truth, and our life.

In his letter to the Christian community in Rome, Paul introduced himself as an apostle, called to deliver a message from God—the gospel, in other words, the risen Christ. The community, Paul emphasized, is beloved by God and called to be holy, consecrated, or set apart to continue the ministry of Jesus (Rom 1:1–7).

In the Gospel according to Matthew, Mary was pregnant with a child by the power of the Spirit. Joseph, already engaged to Mary, faced a dilemma. If the baby wasn't Joseph's, it was logical to conclude that Mary must have committed adultery, which was punishable by death according to custom. But Joseph wasn't about to let that happen. What should he do?

Then Joseph had a dream, an overpowering experience of the divine, that convinced him to take Mary as his wife (Mt 1:18–24).

As I thought about Joseph's dream in this gospel, I thought of the dreams of married couples when they first learn they will be parents. They usually begin to dream about their child.

Their first dreams are usually for a safe birth, a healthy child. And then parents may dream that their sons or daughters will excel in various fields. They may even dare to dream of a star athlete, rock star, or investment "mover and shaker" on Wall Street.

But along the way, these dreams may change very quickly. While they once dreamed about a Nobel Prize winner, Mom and Dad may now settle for their child passing mathematics. Or their dream of a star athlete may quickly be forgotten as they wait and hope that their child will recover from a terrible accident. Or their dream of a high-tech CEO success story may all but disappear when Mom and Dad desperately pray that their child will recover from an addiction of one kind or another.

Joseph in today's gospel must have had dreams for his family as well. But most importantly, the angel assured Joseph that he shouldn't be afraid to take his beloved Mary as his wife.

And as I think about Joseph's dreams, I also think of the dreams of so many of us.

But as Joseph learned from his dreams, the most important things we can dream for our family are these—that they always will know we love them dearly, that we accept them unconditionally for who they are, that we're always ready to forgive them of their peccadilloes, and that we are always praying that they will experience God's love and peace in their daily lives.

Joseph is truly a model of trust in God for us, a man who treated everyone fairly.

Like Joseph, we pray that God will gift us with the eyes of faith to see God in all things, especially in the ordinariness of everyday life. Like Joseph, we pray that God will gift us with his love to accept people as a gift from God, even if they're not quite the gift we would like.

And like Joseph, we pray that God will gift us with the courage always to try to do the right thing, to be a source of affirmation and support to other people, especially our families, our colleagues at work, and our neighbors in the community.

And until Jesus comes again in great power and glory, our purpose in life is to continue doing all the good we can for all the people we can for as long as can—helping those who doubt to find faith, those who despair to find hope, those who are weak to find courage, those who are sick to find health, those who are sad and depressed to find joy, those who wander to find their way back to God, those who are angry to find a way to let go of their anger, and those who are dying to find mercy and peace in God forever.

The Nativity of the Lord

M erry Christmas! *Feliz Navidad! Joyeux Noël! Buon Natale! Frohe Weihnachten!*

During the holidays, there are many family customs, such as singing carols, seeing *The Nutcracker*, listening to the *Messiah*, visiting family and friends, and enjoying meals together.

And as I focus on the true meaning of Christmas, "God with us," I think of children and the clever things they say.

For example, a mother was making pancakes for her two little boys. The brothers began squabbling over who was going to get the first pancake. Mom saw an opportunity to teach her little boys a lesson. "You know, if Jesus was here, he'd say, 'My brother can have the first pancake.'" The five-year-old turned to the three-year-old and said, "Okay. You be Jesus."

The moral of the story is that there's more than one way to get what you want.

Every year we relive the wonderful Christmas story in the liturgy.

The story tells us of a baby in a trough. Of a mother holding her child in her arms as her husband Joseph stays near. Of angels singing and of shepherds running over the hillside to tell the child they love him.

The Gospel according to John sums up this magnificent story in a single line—"The Word became flesh" (Jn 1:1–18).

That line takes us in our imaginations to the beginning of the human family in Genesis. Man and woman walked with God and had friendship with God and one another. Somehow, they lost that friendship, and they fell from grace. Genesis describes that fall very simply yet very graphically. They hid from God, one blamed the other, and even the earthly elements worked against them.

But God didn't leave us to our worse selves. Remember the words of the prophet Isaiah. "Can a mother forget her infant? … Even should she forget, I will never forget you." (Isa 49:15) And so continued the biblical story of salvation.

Amid all ancient Israel's triumphs and tragedies, fortunes and misfortunes, fidelities and infidelities to the covenant, God never reneged on his promises. And so the Word became flesh and made his dwelling among us.

The word of God for the Christmas liturgies is like a prism, through which is refracted the multiple facets of this great mystery of the incarnation. God become one of us.

Isaiah proclaimed glad tidings. The people who walked in darkness had seen a great light (Isa 52:7–10). Paul wrote that the grace of God appeared in Jesus Christ, who made us "heirs" to the promise of eternal life (Heb 1:1–6).

In the Gospel according to Luke, the Virgin Mary gave birth to her

Son. She wrapped him in swaddling clothes and laid him in a manger. The Gospel of John sums up the meaning of Christmas—the Word became flesh. That is God's greatest gift to us.

As I was looking for additional holiday inspiration, I came across a wonderful quote that captures the spirit of Christmas and wraps it all up in a gift we can keep giving throughout the year. While gadgets, games, and trips are all wonderful presents, Ralph Waldo Emerson noted, "The only gift is a portion of one's self." That's more precious to those we love.

First, there is the gift of time. In this busy world, we often don't take time to give of ourselves to others. A phone call to a friend in need, a visit to an ailing or aging relative, a little more time for parents, children, or spouses—these are examples of giving ourselves to others for enjoyment, education, and love.

The second is the gift of a good example. This demonstrates that we respect others, that we are compassionate, that we're a friend, and that we're fair and honest. That we're men and women of integrity is the gift of example for others, especially the young.

The third is the gift of seeing the best in people. Let people know you see them for their positive qualities—and sure enough, they will bring out the best in them.

These psychological gifts cost nothing, but their effects can last a lifetime.

Now let's go back to Christmas and the phrase that magnificently sums it up—"The Word became flesh."

That reality changed our destiny. Christmas means not simply God in Bethlehem of Judea centuries ago but God within us. We carry within ourselves Emmanuel, God with us. How? We do so initially by virtue of the life-giving waters of baptism, by living a life of virtue.

We gather to proclaim the awesome word of God, to celebrate the presence of the living Christ, body and blood, soul and divinity, in this liturgy. For we are by grace what Jesus Christ is by nature, sons and daughters of God our Father, heirs to the kingdom of God.

And that great truth of our faith, God within us, ought to always challenge us to be a good finder, someone who looks for the good in themselves, in other people, and in every situation.

Look for the good in yourself! Remember that magnificent hymn of the Virgin Mary. "My soul proclaims the greatness of the Lord; my spirit rejoices in God my savior. Because the mighty one has done great things for me."

Mary rejoiced in the gifts God had given her, and so too should we rejoice in the gifts God has given us.

Second, look for the good in other people. Someone wrote that people in many ways are like wildflowers. If you have ever studied a wildflower carefully, you'll see the delicate veins, the fragile petals, and the beautiful blossom. If you turn the flower to the sunlight, you discover its special symmetry. The wildflower has a beauty all its own. And so too do people.

And finally, look for good in all situations of life. When one door closes, another door inevitably opens if we pay close enough attention.

And who is the ultimate good finder? God so loved us that he became one of us.

Yes, Jesus had a unique relationship. He was one with God. He is a God-man, a healer, a teacher, and a peacemaker. Think of all the people in the Gospels Jesus met—the blind, the leper, the lame, the sinner, the forgotten. And Jesus found goodness in all of them where many didn't.

The promised Messiah has come. He is in our midst sacramentally and mystically, and he will come again in glory and power at the end-time.

In the meantime, here is our Christmas challenge:

> What better season for wrongs to be righted, and friends
> to be reunited;
> for new dreams to start …
> What better season for mending and healing, for saying
> and feeling
> what's in the heart.
> What better season for love to keep glowing, for hope
> to start growing,
> for troubles to cease.
> What better season for sharing and giving,
> for once again living in joy and in peace!

MARY, THE HOLY MOTHER
OF GOD (NEW YEAR)

How many have read predictions for the new year? Here are some: The president will moderate his pledges, the price of oil will increase, the euro will crash, and the Buccaneers will win the Super Bowl. Now that's one prediction I wouldn't bet on.

If you find these predictions bothersome, here's a consolation: often the forecasters have been wrong. Remember the predictions about Brexit and the election? So much for predictions.

But you may be wondering what the new year will be like. Everywhere there seems to be change—political, economic, moral, scientific, and religious. Yes, there's so much grandeur and yet so much misery on the planet. The future seems to offer as many possibilities of death as it does of life.

To some extent, we may be our own worst enemies. We have freed ourselves from so many tyrannies, especially in the Group of 20 central bank governors—for example, poverty, disease, and illiteracy—only to create new tyrannies—for example, the spread of nuclear arms.

Perhaps we might want to make this prayer our mantra in the new year: "God, grant me the serenity to accept the things I cannot change, courage to change the things I can, and the wisdom to know the difference. Living one day at a time; enjoying one moment at a time … trusting that God will make all things right … that I might be reasonably happy in this life and supremely happy with God forever in the next."

That prayer can be an anchor as a new, unpredictable global order begins to take shape.

But how should we respond to the shape of the future? There's only one Christian response: hope. Let me explain why.

I heard about a father who buried his son, killed in a car crash. As the coffin was lowered into the grave, the distraught father whispered to a close friend, "It can't end like this. Please! It just can't end like this!" The friend reassured the father that because of Jesus's resurrection and his son's faith in Christ, the son was already in the presence of God in a new kind of spiritual embodiment. "One day," the friend continued, "we all will be together again for eternity."

As we begin the year, we may be wondering, *Will darkness and evil prevail? Will random violence and reckless wars persist? Will depression continue robbing people of joy? Does it have to end like this?* With faith in Jesus Christ, it most certainly doesn't have to end like this.

Many people today put their hope in wealth, a successful career, or a long-term relationship. There's nothing wrong with any of these things—but none of them is a solid enough foundation on which to anchor one's life.

Hope isn't just a feeling or emotion. It's not dependent on circumstances. Real hope is a constant positive attitude that, no matter the circumstances, things will change for the better.

The horizon for Christian hope is Jesus Christ shall come again in great glory and power, and we look for the coming of the Lord. That horizon is what makes it possible to be hopeful and therefore to find life meaningful in what we do and how we live.

At the very core of Christianity is the central reality that Jesus appeared alive to the disciples after his death. The tomb was empty. There were many appearances. By the power of the Spirit, God transfigured the earthly Jesus into a new kind of spiritual embodiment. And one day we, like the risen Christ, would make an evolutionary leap in the mystery of death into a similar kind of spiritual embodiment.

Christian hope is the conviction that the universe in which we live has ultimate meaning, that Christ in his Second Coming will bring to completion the process of transformation begun in his resurrection. And that is why hope is a fundamental characteristic of the Christian life. And with that hope, we can gaze into the future with a positive attitude.

Today is the Feast of Mary, the Mother of God. The word of God from the book of Numbers highlights a magnificent blessing. "May the Lord bless and keep you! The Lord let his face shine upon you, and be gracious to you. The Lord look upon you kindly and give you peace!" (Nm 6:22–27). That is also my prayer for all of us this year.

In his letter to the Christian community in Galatia, central Turkey, Paul proclaimed that we are sons and daughters of God our Father, coheirs to the kingdom of God. Yes, we are called to live lives worthy of our new status as adopted children of God (Gal 4:4–7).

In the Gospel according to Luke, we have the shepherds or bedouins giving homage to the Christ child and shouting their amazing experience everywhere they could. And then Mary and Joseph named their child Jesus, which means "God saves." He is indeed our Savior: our way, our truth, and our eternal life (Lk 2:16–21).

Mary is truly the model of discipleship for all of us as we begin the new year. And what made Mary a disciple? In the Gospel according to Luke, the author said that God mysteriously broke into her life and asked Mary to believe she would bear within herself an extraordinary child. But the author went on to say that Mary "was quite perplexed" by this. God revealed very little to Mary—the basic call, the bare bones. God simply asked Mary for faith or trust in his mighty word. God didn't promise Mary the so-called good life; he simply promised to be with Mary always in her moments of joy and sorrow.

And Mary simply said, "Let it happen to me as you say."

These words—"Let it happen to me as you say"—tell us what discipleship is all about. We can very easily say these words when everything is going our way, so to speak. Problems arise only when what is happening to us isn't what we want to happen or when what is happening to us is the opposite of what we want (for example, a life-threatening illness, an unexpected death, a job loss, or a broken relationship).

And so we, like Mary, will be quite perplexed many times as we go through the cycle of our own human development from adolescence through young adulthood to old age. Yet despite our perplexity at times, the ongoing call to discipleship demands a ceaseless faith. God will always be near us, closer to us than we are to ourselves. And God will work his wonders in us as he did in Mary. And in faith we will be able to sing the song of Mary. "My soul proclaims the greatness [the glory] of the Lord."

I conclude with some favorite New Year resolutions that are worth repeating.

The greatest joy... Giving

The greatest "shot in the arm"......................... Encouragement

The most powerful force in life....................…....…... Love

The worst thing to be without........................... Hope

The greatest asset.. Faith

The most prized possession............................. Integrity

The most contagious spirit............................. Enthusiasm

The most powerful communication.................. Prayer

Second Sunday in Ordinary Time

Y ears ago, a mentor advised me to be careful about what I say "because it could come back to bite you."

He cited a story about an army general who prattled on and on at a ceremony. A young second lieutenant muttered to the woman alongside him, "What an insufferable windbag that guy is." The woman replied, "Lieutenant, do you know who I am?" "No, ma'am." "I am the wife of that general you called an insufferable windbag." The lieutenant said, "Ma'am, do you know who I am?" "No," said the general's wife. "Thank

God," said the lieutenant, and he quickly disappeared into the crowd. The point is, be careful what you say.

Do you notice anything different in the church? The Christmas crèche, lights, and poinsettias are gone. In the liturgical calendar we are now in "ordinary time," and the word of God invites us to reflect on what it means to be a disciple of Jesus, our master.

In writings from Isaiah, Paul, and John today, we hear various titles ascribed to Jesus. He is the "lamb" who saves us through his death and resurrection, the "Son" who is one with the God of Israel. He is the "Christ," St. Paul said, the long-expected Messiah who inaugurates the kingdom of God. He is the sovereign "Lord," to whom we profess our ultimate allegiance. He is the "servant," Isaiah wrote, the "light" who illumines the answers to the fundamental questions of life.

Yes, the word of God ascribes several titles to Jesus. The one that stands out for me is John's—"Behold, the lamb of God." When John saw Jesus on the banks of the Jordan River, Jesus changed John's life forever. Jesus, the sacrificial lamb, was about to open up to us new dimensions of life beyond death.

Can you think of an experience that changed your life, an experience that made you see things differently? Let me tell you about the experience of Helen Keller, a twentieth-century educator, journalist, humanitarian, and inspiration to many. Helen Keller overcame physical obstacles most of us can't imagine. Although blind, she was a visionary. Although deaf, she listened with her heart. She noted that no pessimist ever discovered the secrets of the stars, sailed to an uncharted land, or opened a new haven to the human spirit.

Despite her handicaps, Helen developed a positive can-do attitude that helped her discover a world full of possibilities. In her autobiography, *The Story of My Life*, she wrote about the day the outside world broke into the closed world of this six-year-old. She'd been born healthy but was stricken with a virus that left her deaf and blind at nineteen months. The catalyst was water, an essential element of life related to what John in today's gospel was doing: baptizing.

Helen described the experience that changed her life. "My teacher, Anne Sullivan, placed my hand under the spout. And as the cool stream of water gushed over one hand, she spelled into the other hand the word water, first slowly, then rapidly. And then suddenly ... somehow the mystery of language was revealed to me. I knew then that w-a-t-e-r meant the wonderful cool something that was flowing over my hand ... I left the well-house eager to learn."

Yes, everything has a name.

Now, think of our own rebirth in the waters of baptism. We not only experienced water, but through that water we became disciples of Jesus. That experience changed our lives. In "the wonderful, cool something," the life of God became ours.

Helen Keller's experience of water was the beginning of a new journey for her, and so too our baptism is the beginning of our own journey to the eternal dwelling place of God, with Jesus as our mentor, teacher, and companion.

The author of Isaiah took us back in our imaginations to the sixth century before Jesus, to the Jews exiled in Babylonia. This passage is a poem, a song about the vocation of a "servant of God" who will bring hope to a people who have lost hope. This "servant" renews God's covenant with the Jews and through them pours out God's life on all peoples. He will be a "light" to all (Isa 49:3, 5–6). The Christian community sees in this "servant" Jesus, whose vocation or calling was to be our way, our truth, life, and light in our journey toward our heavenly dwelling place (1 Cor 1:1–3).

In the gospel, John pointed out Jesus as the Lamb of God, an allusion to the lamb in the Passover meal and the sacrificial lamb in temple worship. John also saw Jesus coming up out of the Jordan waters, and the Spirit of God confirming Jesus as "Son of God" (Jn 1:29–34).

Now what was John's vocation or calling? It was simply to point to Jesus as the Messiah. As we reflect on John's vocation, we might ask ourselves whether we, by virtue of who we are and what we do, point to Jesus.

And what was John doing in the Jordan? He was baptizing and inviting people to repent, to orient their lives to God and the things of God. And isn't this what baptism does?

To begin with, baptism is a gift from God and a rite of initiation into a worldwide community of disciples.

Why be baptized? We first must understand who we are in relationship to God. At birth, we lack God's life within us. That really is what original sin means, a lack of something—a lack of a relationship with God. The book of Genesis captures this lack very simply yet graphically. Man and woman fell out of their relationship or friendship with God. How? We really don't know.

But then God became flesh in Jesus of Nazareth. God through the bloody death and glorious resurrection of Jesus by the power of the Spirit reestablished that relationship with God. In his letter to the Christian community at Corinth, a seaport city in Greece, Paul explained that God through Jesus by the power of the Spirit has made us God's adopted sons and daughters. Yes, God became one of us so we might become like God.

That's an incredible gift. That's why Paul urged us to live holy lives worthy of our status. Wouldn't we like God to say about us, "This is my beloved son or beloved daughter, with whom I am well pleased"?

Through baptism, we enter a relationship with God through a community of fellow disciples.

In early Christianity, candidates were often immersed in water. Water symbolizes life and death. A hurricane can demonstrate how life threatening water can be, and water on a 100-degree-plus day can easily show how life giving it can be.

The early Christian candidate stepped down into the water and then came up, symbolizing a dying to a self-centered life and a rising to a God-centered or others-centered life with God. By the eleventh century, a millennium after John the Baptist, pouring water on the head became the common baptismal practice.

But now let's go back to the one question we might ask ourselves. Do we point to Jesus through who we are and what we do? And if we don't, when will we?

THIRD SUNDAY IN ORDINARY TIME

I played a "men over 60" basketball game in a New York City athletic club during the Christmas holidays. Believe it or not, we didn't have to jump for the ball. The referee simply put the ball on the floor, and whoever could bend over and pick it up first got possession. Now that's my kind of game.

The word of God today gives us Isaiah, Paul, and Jesus. They lived purpose-driven lives, to use the title of Rick Warren's best seller. Pope John Paul II captured the crux of that book more precisely in this paraphrase—it is no accident that we are here.

Each and every human person has been created in the image and likeness of God. We have within us the capacities for wisdom and virtue. With these gifts and God's grace, we can build a civilization worthy of the human person. That's a powerful statement about purpose.

In their hearts, people want to live for something greater than themselves that can give ultimate meaning to their lives. This quest takes different forms in different people. Perhaps it's a commitment to family, health care, education, human rights, a cleaner environment, freedom, and safety—to name but a few causes. When a person finds something that gives transcendent meaning to his or her life, it awakens new energies. People become true believers, so to speak.

Isaiah, Paul, and Jesus had faith in an all-good, sovereign God; they heard God's call and responded with a wholehearted yes. They knew who they were and what their mission was in life. They realized God had committed some work to them. They asked, "If I don't do it, who will? If I don't do it now, when shall I do it?" Their lives couldn't be a failure because they found meaning beyond this transitory world. To quote the letter of John, "This is the victory that overcomes the world, our faith" (1 Jn 5:4).

Today's word takes us back in our imaginations to the eighth century before Jesus, to a man named Isaiah. Ancient Assyria was on the march against the northern kingdom of Israel. In the midst of this, Isaiah spoke about the future. A great light, a king, would illuminate the darkness that now enveloped the anxious Hebrews; this king would trust completely in God, not in fickle alliances with foreign powers. And he would free the Hebrews from their oppressors (Isa 8:23–9:3).

Isaiah challenged us always to trust in God's unconditional love for us despite the problems and disappointments we may face. God is always close to us. He won't give us more than we can handle.

In his letter to the Christian community at Corinth in Greece, Paul deplored the divisions that seemed to be tearing the community apart (1 Cor 1:10–13, 17).

Paul begged for unity in the community in light of its common bond. They were God's adopted sons and daughters. They are all one family.

Today, of course, it doesn't seem as though we are one family. Everywhere we find dysfunctional relationships. Paul, if he were her today, probably would advise us to keep our tempers, share the blame, and make the best of the situation, since most things in life seldom work out perfectly. That's good advice for all of us.

In the Gospel according to Matthew, the author proclaimed that Jesus is the fulfillment of the prophecies of Isaiah. He is the anointed one, the Christos, who will bring light into our darkness by proclaiming the good news. God has become one of us in Jesus of Nazareth so we can become like God. Therefore, Jesus exhorts us to orient your life to God and the things of God. The kingdom of heaven is at hand. And then Jesus began to call some highly unlikely people to discipleship, ordinary fishermen (Mt 4:12–23).

We are in the middle of the week of prayer for Christian unity. Why? Because Jesus prayed at the Last Supper that his disciples "may all be one as you, Father, are in me and I in you."

But are the 2.2 billion Christians one? We, in fact, are a divided

Christianity. We've marked the five hundredth anniversary of Martin Luther's clarion call for reform in the church. Luther initially argued for reform, not division. But his call spread like a contagion across Europe and launched Protestant Christianity.

Today we have about 1.2 billion Catholics, 800 million Protestants, and 260 million Orthodox. And until Angelo Roncalli was elected Pope John XXIII in 1958, Catholics and Protestants generally emphasized what divided them.

Pope John XXIII created a transformation, especially in Catholic-Protestant relations. He moved Christians from diatribe to dialogue with his affable, friendly, and lovable personality; and his sense of humor. For example, a reporter asked the pope how many people work in the Vatican. "About half," replied the pontiff.

Good Pope John realized that before people can discuss what divides them, they must get to know one another. This search for unity reached a milestone among Catholics with the 1964 promulgation of the "Decree on Ecumenism," which encourages conversations with our separated brothers and sisters about what unites and divides us and how we can cooperate, especially in humanitarian projects.

Catholics are linked with mainstream Christian churches in many ways: through a common creed, baptism, the Bible, and many justice and peace issues. But Christians are still divided on key issues—for example, the authority of the pope. But together we must find ways beyond what divides us to what unites us.

And so we pray this week that we might all be one—open to conversations with other Christian traditions and at the same time faithful to our Catholic tradition.

Today Pope Francis wants us to be a church that welcomes people, saints as well as sinners. He wants us to be a compassionate church, always reformable, serving one another, especially the poor and vulnerable, open to dialogue with people of faith and of no faith.

We are a worldwide community of believers—multinational and multicolored—that remembers Jesus, a community of disciples that hears God speak to us in the liturgy of the Word and in the liturgy of the Eucharist. It presents the risen Christ sacramentally and mystically in the bread and wine. The risen Christ is really and truly among us.

And yes, we are a community that takes a stand on peace and justice. The worldwide Catholic community sponsors and staffs shelters, hospices, soup kitchens, literacy programs, day care centers, hospitals, and schools throughout the world. And hundreds of Catholic relief and refugee agencies attempt to meet the basic needs of the poor.

But alas, we are also a community of believers with tensions. Why is that so? Because we are humans, saints as well as sinners. Some people are messy and make a mess out of things, and so, like many other things in life, we must live with some messiness and muddle through as best we can.

As we pray for Christian unity, let us give thanks to God for the faith community to which we belong, a community that calls us to a life with God here today, and to an indescribable heavenly life where we shall be like God and see God as he really is. Amen.

Fourth Sunday in Ordinary Time

A new pastor went out one day to visit his parishioners. All went well until he came to one house. It was clear someone was home, but no one answered the door. Finally, the pastor took out his business card, wrote "Revelation 3:20" on it, and stuck the card on the door. Revelation 3:20 reads, "Behold, I stand at the door and knock. If anyone hears my voice and opens the door, then I will enter … and dine."

A week later, the pastor received his card back with a quotation written below his. "Genesis 3:10," which reads, "And man answered: 'I heard you in the garden; but I was afraid, because I was naked, so I hid.'" Now there's a sense of humor.

The word of God takes us back in our imaginations to the seventh century before Jesus to a man named Zephaniah. Ancient Assyria had conquered the northern kingdom of Israel and made a satellite of the southern kingdom. But now Babylonia was emerging as the new Middle East superpower (Zep 2:3; 3:12–13).

The author of Zephaniah challenged the Hebrews, in light of this new threat, to seek God in their daily lives. How? By being faithful to their covenant promises, fair in their dealings with one another, and acknowledging their absolute dependence on an all-good sovereign God. Perhaps God would then protect them from Babylonia.

But then the author dramatically changed the scene in the second sentence from danger to deliverance. Yes, some Hebrews, a remnant, will survive; they will acknowledge God, walk in the ways of the covenant, and live in peace.

The author invited us, creatures who came out of nothingness, to be humble and grateful to an all-good God for who we are and what we have.

In his letter to the Christian community in Corinth, Paul reminded them that they are people with neither intellectual heft nor political clout, little to nothing to brag about. But God chose them. God does wondrous things through the least likely people to demonstrate that the power of God is at work. Paul then added that Jesus is our true wisdom, our sole redeemer and sanctifier (1 Cor 1:26–31).

Paul urged us to let people see the power of God at work in our lives.

In the Gospel according to Matthew, Jesus described what it means to be disciples. They recognize who they are (mere creatures of an allmighty creator); they seek God in their daily lives; they forgive wrongs done to them; they are peacemakers, bridge builders; and yes, they are ready to do the right thing. The beatitudes are indeed a splendid spirituality for all ages (Mt 5:1–12).

Jesus in the beatitudes calls us to do surprising things to live by spiritual rather than material values. He wants us to attach ourselves to the things of God, to find our joy and purpose in service to others, to seek what is right in all things, to be compassionate and forgiving, to stop and listen to God's voice speaking in the quiet of our hearts, to work for peace in our homes and communities, and to invest what we have and are in bringing about the kingdom of God in our own time and place.

What does that mean concretely?

If you do something for someone else for no other reason than to bring joy to people's lives, and if you put yourself second for the needs of another, blessed are you.

If you do the "right" thing when the conventional wisdom is to do the "smart" thing, forgive someone for wrongs done to you and move forward, and stop and spend even just a moment thinking about all the good in your life and find yourself feeling a sense of gratitude, blessed are you.

If you can defuse someone's anger, bridge a chasm between you and another, bring a positive perspective to an otherwise-negative situation, and endure a negative look from someone because you took a stand based on what was morally and ethically right, blessed are you.

In the blessings you give, you have been blessed.

Each of us is mortal. I don't want to be morbid, but it's true—we are going to die. We don't know when or how, but we do know we will die.

Now, when was the last time you stopped to think about your life? The fact of death should make us think about what we will do and how we will live. If your doctor told you, "You probably have about six months to live," you would live very differently. That's why it's spiritually healthy to reflect on our mortality. It generally rearranges priorities.

Most people get no warning. But if your doctor gives a time frame and you think about living and dying, you have the benefit of getting your affairs in order and the opportunity of bidding farewell to those you love. With that news, we quickly sort out the important things from what's not so important.

There's an ancient wisdom that says God sends each person into this life with a special message to deliver, a special song to sing for others, and a special act of love to bestow. Perhaps this prayer can be our message and song and act of love.

> In a world full of sadness, may we be people full of gladness …
> In a world that complains, may we be people that care …
> In a world that's out of tune, may we be people full of harmony …
> In a world full of war, may we be people full of peace …
> In a world full of crime, may we be people full of honesty …
> In a world full of heartache, may we be people full of hope …
> and in a discouraged world, may we be people full of encouragement.

I conclude with experiences from hospice nurses. Someone asked these nurses, "When people are dying, what do they talk about?" The nurses said people who are dying often speak to them about how they wish they had lived differently. For example,

I wish I had spent more time with the people I love.

I wish I had been a better spouse.

I wish I had discovered my purpose earlier.

I wish I had quit my job and found something I really enjoyed doing.

I wish I hadn't spent so much time chasing the wrong things.

These were the regrets of people finishing their time on this earth. Each of them contains a powerful lesson for those of us who are still living. The point is this: It's healthy to think about mortality from time to time. It puts things in perspective and reminds us of what truly matters.

Someone wrote, "Twenty years from now we will be more disappointed by the things we didn't do than by the ones we did." Think about it. Live a life of no regrets.

The perspective that death is inevitable may compel us to reorder our priorities and live lives of the beatitudes. The goal isn't gloom and doom but rather to focus on our deeply held values, to celebrate the joy and purpose of the gift of life. And that gift of life is important for people of all ages and stages to celebrate. Don't regret a moment.

FIFTH SUNDAY IN ORDINARY TIME

A quick survey! How many will be watching the Super Bowl? How many are rooting for the Patriots? The Falcons?

I begin with a story about a rural monastery in the Midwest. The abbess was dying, and all the nuns were gathered around her bedside. One gave the abbess a glass of milk with plenty of brandy in it to ease her pain. The abbess took a sip and suddenly perked up. Another nun asked for the abbess's dying words. The abbess took a really big gulp of the brandy and milk, smiled, and said, "Don't sell that cow." Now that's a businesswoman.

Today's word of God speaks about salt and light. How many have said someone is "the salt of the earth"? The phrase usually means someone is dependable, one you can count on through thick and thin." Or a sailor might say the captain's speech is "salty"; that is coarse, not politically correct.

Did anyone ever eat a handful of salt? Or drink a glass of ocean water? I hope not. Salt by itself doesn't taste very good—it might even make you sick. And did anyone ever look directly at the sun or into a bright light bulb? I hope not. Doing so can severely damage your eyes.

Salt and sun, in and of themselves, aren't very useful. But when you add salt to food or shine light on artwork, they both can do wonders.

Salt can bring out the natural flavor in food, from filet mignon to popcorn. Salt in our bodies enables our muscles to contract, our blood to circulate, and our hearts to beat. In short, salt enhances, purifies, and preserves.

And light can transform a cold night into a warm day. Light enables us to study, discover, and behold the beauty and wonders of God's universe. Light warms, nurtures, sustains, reveals, and cheers.

Jesus asks us to be the "salt of the earth," the "light of the world." We are salt when we bring out the best in people. We are light when we illuminate the presence of God all around us. To become salt is to bring out the "flavor" of God in everyone and everything, and to be light means to illuminate the presence of God amid everyday life.

The word of God first takes us back to the sixth century before Jesus, to a collection of writings in the book of the prophet Isaiah. In this passage, many Jews returned to their homeland from Babylonia only to become disillusioned by the harsh realities they had to face, like many Syrians today. And so the Jews proclaimed a national fast to ask for God's favor.

But the author here noted that fasting is useless if we treat people unfairly or deny their basic human rights. It's better, the author said, to practice what we call the corporal works of mercy. Feed the hungry, shelter the homeless, care for the sick, and be compassionate. If you do these things, to reference today's scripture, your light will break forth like the dawn (Isa 58:7–10).

Paul said to the Christian community in Corinth that God's power was at work within him, even though he went about his ministry in "fear and trembling." Paul asked us to look for the wisdom of God—not in people of eloquence but in the Spirit, who empowers us to proclaim the good news. God became one of us in Jesus of Nazareth so we could become like God. That indeed is our purpose in life—to become like God (1 Cor 2:1–5).

In the Gospel according to Matthew, Jesus said we are to be the "salt of the earth" and the "light of the world" to others. But how can we be salt that brings out the best in people? And how can we be light that illuminates the presence of God all around us? By who we are and what we do with what we have (Mt 5:13–16).

Each of us has gifts or talents that can bring out the best in other people. You and I possess by virtue of baptism the power of God to believe, hope, and love. And within our society there are many splendid callings. Father or mother, teacher or student, doctor or lawyer or businessperson—whoever you are, you have a specific vocation, a calling, right now to bring out the best in other people so they will choose the better version of themselves.

How do we do this? By asking the Spirit of God to work within us. Oh, yes, personality can be a blessing; it's great if we easily warm up to people. But more importantly, the Spirit of God works through us as we are. The Spirit of God illumines our minds to know the way we should behave and strengthens us to do so despite obstacles. He gives us his gifts—wisdom to focus on what truly matters; understanding and knowledge to enter the mysteries of God; counsel to make good moral decisions; fortitude to stand up for what's right; piety to give God our praise and worship; and fear of the Lord, the healthy concern never to lose our friendship with God. The Spirit gives us these gifts so we can be salt and light.

The gifts or talents we have aren't for ourselves but for others, for the family where we live, the workplace where we interface with colleagues, and the community where we meet neighbors. The gifts we have look beyond ourselves to our lives with others. No Christian is an island. The Spirit empowers us as we are to help others choose the better version of themselves and to become more godlike in their relationships with other people.

I conclude with some wisdom from one of my favorite presidents, Theodore Roosevelt. Historians feature him as one of our four transformational presidents alongside Washington, Lincoln, and Franklin D. Roosevelt. Teddy Roosevelt based his philosophy of life on what he called "realizable ideals," such as, "keep your eyes on the stars and your feet on the ground." "Speak softly and carry a big stick; you will go far." And, "It is not the critic who counts, but the doer in the arena."

Some have accused Teddy Roosevelt of platitudes. But as one author said, "A brick is a platitude, but lay one brick upon another, according to a grand design, and behold, a cathedral." Teddy Roosevelt believed that you "found yourself" by being involved with institutions, people, jobs, causes, movements, and everyday life. He urged us to become the person "who strives valiantly ... who spends himself on a worthy cause; who at best knows the triumph of high achievement, and who at worst, if he fails, at least fails while daring greatly so that his place will never be with those cold and timid souls who know neither victory nor defeat."

Yes, each of us, with the gifts of the Spirit working within us, can be salt and light to others by who we are and what we do with what we have.

Sixth Sunday in Ordinary Time

A husband said to his wife, "When I die, I want you to put all my money in my casket. I'm taking it with me." The wife surprisingly said she would. Soon after, the husband died. And the wife, just as the casket was about to close, placed a strongbox in it. Her friend gasped, "I hope you weren't crazy enough to put all his money in the casket." "Yes, I first put all his money into my account and then put a check in the box." Now that's one-upmanship!

The word of God carries us back in our imaginations to the wisdom literature of ancient Israel, the book of Sirach, a collection of advice about how to live well. This book may even have inspired William Bennett's *The Book of Virtues* because the biblical author described the good life in terms of virtue: a simple lifestyle, self-discipline, responsibility, honesty, forgiveness, courage, compassion, persistence, and faith in God.

In this passage, the author noted that we must choose between life and death, right and wrong, truth and falsehood. These choices will lead us on a pathway either to salvation or to damnation. But no matter how we choose, God ultimately is in control (Sir 15:15–20).

The passage asks us to pray for God's grace to try to do the right thing every day.

In his letter to the Christian community in Corinth, Greece, St. Paul wrote about true wisdom—that is, Jesus Christ. The risen Christ is *the* revelation of God to us. Everything God ever wanted to do for us or say to us, God did and said in Jesus Christ by the power of the Spirit

(1 Cor 2:6–10). Paul invited us always to look to Jesus as our true wisdom and let his life and ministry be a guide for ours.

In the Gospel according to Matthew, Jesus described what it means to be a disciple. Jesus employed four antitheses or opposites ("you have heard ... but I say") to emphasize the importance of attitude over legalese. Jesus here used a bit of Middle Eastern hyperbole to make his point. Our attitudes create our behaviors. And if we have bad attitudes, we surely will behave badly.

Jesus then gave four examples. Here is one instance. "You have heard that it was said, you shall not murder; but I say to you: you shall not be angry." Why? Because a bad attitude, anger or resentment, can seethe into bad behavior, verbal or even worse, physical abuse. Discipleship with Jesus calls for a change of heart, a change of attitude, thinking and feeling positively, not negatively (Mt 5:17–37).

I would like to take my cue from Paul's letter and focus on Jesus as our true wisdom. He is our exemplar, our guide, our leader about how to live well. And Jesus also challenges us to be an exemplar, guide, or leader for others.

First, who is Jesus? He is one with God, a God-man who is completely divine and completely human. God became one of us so we could become like God. Jesus experienced, as we do, hunger, joy, friendship, disappointment, loneliness, and death. He was a rabbi, a teacher, a prophet, a wonder worker; he was eventually crucified but then raised up and transfigured into a new kind of spiritual embodiment. And this risen Christ is alive in our midst, especially in the sacramental signs of our Catholic community. And because he is alive, we too are alive with God's life and favor.

Jesus is indeed our wisdom, guide, and leader. For me, a leader has a sense of purpose, generates trust, communicates hope, and translates vision into results. Jesus communicated purpose through words, signs, and wonders in a way that galvanized, energized, and excited people. He generated trust among his disciples, which was the glue that bound them together in their commitments. He inspired hope in the crowds, with a clear vision of the future, life in relationship with God forever.

Finally, Jesus converted vision into action through his death and resurrection.

Matthew 23:10 advises, in so many words, that there is only one master, one Messiah, one life leader, one life coach: Jesus Christ. This Jesus calls each of us to be guides and leaders in our own situations. Yes, to be called by God to influence others—that's leadership—is an enormous privilege, but it carries with it great responsibility.

We must possess two things: confidence and character. Jesus possessed these in full.

Not only confidence in ourselves but, first and foremost, confidence in God. The psalmists had that kind of confidence. God was their shield, strength, and guide.

Second, we must be men and women of character. If you look at the leadership failures in this country in the last one hundred years, I guess you'll find that 99 percent weren't failures in competence; they were failures in character. Greed, lying, intolerance, immorality, amorality—these are all character failures. Leadership involves ethics, right and wrong, a sense of responsibility, a value system, integrity. That's why character counts. David Brooks makes that very point in his best seller, *The Road to Character*.

The quality of our lives and our soul's destiny will be measured by our character. That means going the extra mile, helping a fellow human being, being faithful in our relationships and responsibilities, working for the common good, and trusting in a good and compassionate God, who is ever near us and will guide us safely to our heavenly dwelling.

More precisely, we might ask ourselves whether we strive to reflect these attributes of character in our everyday lives. Let me highlight four:

• Integrity

This means practicing what we preach and making sure we lift people up, not pull them down. A humorous example is the famous Abraham Lincoln vs. Stephen Douglas debates in 1858. Douglas accused Lincoln of being two faced. Lincoln replied calmly, "I leave it to my audience: If I had two faces, do you think I would be wearing this one?" Integrity is the opposite of being two faced. Shakespeare put it well: "To thine own self be true."

- Authenticity

  Hypocrites do everything so *others can see them*. But what really matters is who we are when nobody is looking. Think about it. That's doing the right thing, even when nobody is looking.

- Humility

  Jesus warns us not to be bewitched by titles and prominent positions and public flattery. Don't let people put us up on a pedestal. We are all flawed human beings. Jesus said, "For those who exalt themselves will be humbled, and those who humble themselves will be exalted." (Mt 23:12)

- Focus

  This means getting our priorities straight—faithful and responsible in our relationships with God and one another; grateful to God that we are; standing up for what's right; being generous with what we have; and always ready to lend a helping hand to everyone.

  These, for me, are four key attributes of character.

  In light of Paul's focus on Jesus as our true wisdom, our prayer might be, "Lord, help me to live a life of integrity, authenticity, humility, and focus. Help me to have a similar concern for others as Jesus had for us. Give me compassion toward those who are struggling with life's problems. Help me to fix my eyes on our true wisdom, Jesus Christ, and to become like him for others, men and women of confidence and character."

Seventh Sunday in Ordinary Time

I read about a nun who worked for a home health care agency in rural West Virginia. While making her rounds, she ran out of gasoline. As luck would have it, there was an Exxon gas station just down the road. She walked in to buy some gas. The attendant regretfully told her he had just lent the only can he had, but he was sure the fellow would be back shortly.

Since the nun was in a hurry, she looked for something to fill with gas. She spotted a bedpan in her health care supplies. She filled it with gasoline.

As the nun poured the gas from the bedpan into the tank, two Baptists were watching from the roadside, and one said, "If that car starts, I'm definitely becoming a Catholic." What is the moral of the story? It's amazing the many ways we can influence people.

I just came across a new book titled *The Power of Meaning*. People want to feel a sense of well-being on one hand, yet many feel alienated and depressed. Happiness, the author proposes, isn't a goal in life because such a goal is too self-centered. Happiness results from living an others-centered life.

The author, Emily Esfahani Smith, then describes ingredients that will create a meaningful life and result in happiness. First is a sense of belonging, whether family, friends, colleagues, or like-minded pals.

Belonging makes us feel that we matter and that we can be our true selves.

The second ingredient is purpose. Living with a purpose motivates and energizes us to do something for others. It can be our job, volunteer service, or pastime. The third ingredient is—storytelling. We are all storytellers in that we try to make sense out of our lives and form an identity. The final ingredient is transcendence. We try to live for someone or something greater than ourselves.

The point is simple enough. If you have these four ingredients, you will be happy.

Here I would argue that there's a subconscious, if not conscious, quest for what is ultimately true—God in all of us. St. Augustine in the fourth century expressed this: "Our hearts are restless until they rest in you, O God."

Now what does God's word say to us? Jesus in today's gospel asks us to love our enemies. The real challenge is to love the people we live and work with along with relatives and neighbors who annoy us (and whom we probably annoy). "To love our enemies" is to create and nurture a friendly, helpful, and welcoming atmosphere. Jesus in the Gospels instills within us a vision that sees beyond stereotypes, politics, and appearances; it recognizes the "spark of the divine" in everyone, to paraphrase Scott Peck's *The Road Less Traveled*, no matter how "bad" or "unlovable" he or she can seem. In the Greek text of Matthew's Gospel, the word for *love* is *agape*. That indicates not a romantic or emotional love but an unconditional love for our fellow human beings, wishing them not bad luck or misfortune but good.

You don't need to like someone to love him or her. The agape Jesus asks us to have for our enemies means that, no matter how much they injure, hurt, or upset us, we will never let bitterness close our hearts to them; nor will we seek anything but their good. Agape recognizes the humanity we share with all people who call God "Father," and that love begins within our own households, workplaces, and neighborhoods.

Today's word of God first carries us back in our imaginations to the book of Leviticus, one of the first five books in the Hebrew Torah or the Christian Pentateuch. The author's words demand, "Be holy, for I, the Lord your God, am holy." The author then asks us to be compassionate with one another, to "not bear hatred … You shall love your neighbor as yourself." (Lev 19:1–2, 17–18). Because we are created in the image of God, so we ought to reflect Godly behavior in our daily lives.

In his letter to the Christian community at Corinth in Greece, Paul proclaimed that we are a living temple of God. The awesome Spirit of God dwells within us. Worldly wisdom, Paul continued, pales in light of godly wisdom. Paul concluded that all things are ours because we belong to Christ and Christ belongs to God (1 Cor 3:16–23). Paul challenged us to become living temples of God.

In the Gospel according to Matthew, Jesus made some radical demands on us. Love your enemies. If someone slaps you on one side of the face, offer the other. Give to everyone who asks. Do to others as you would have them do to you (Mt 5:38–48).

Now how can anyone practice some of these ethical teachings of Jesus? How can we understand them? Some of these teachings don't seem practical. Who can possibly "give to everyone who asks"? And so, are these teachings simply another example of Middle Eastern hyperbole or exaggeration? A few people—for example, Francis of Assisi or Dorothy Day—have tried to take these teachings literally. But for most people, they're not very practical. So the question remains—how do we understand these ethical teachings?

First, we must remember that Jesus connects our love of God with our love for one another. The judgment scene of Matthew 25 says this truth loudly and clearly—when I was hungry, when I was thirsty, and so forth. We can't say we love God and yet neglect our needy fellow human beings.

Second, these radical ethical teachings of Jesus must be linked to the mission of Jesus.

Jesus proclaimed that the kingdom of God is in our midst. Yes, the kingdom is here, but it's not completely or fully here. You and I are living in between the historical coming of Jesus centuries ago in Bethlehem and the final coming of Jesus in glory at the end-time. We live in the tension between.

Jesus indicates the goal or thrust of our ethical behavior, but this goal may not always be achievable. For example, "giving to everyone who asks" isn't always possible, yet it does indicate the thrust or direction of our lives. Be generous with our time, talent, and treasure.

To the person who strikes you on one side of the face, Jesus said, offer the other as well. But sometimes we must stand up against wrongs; sometimes we must fight against evil—for example, the evil of Nazism. Sometimes we may have to take someone's life in self-defense. But the teaching of Jesus indicates again the thrust or direction of our lives— that is, we should try as often as possible to be peacemakers, healers, bridge builders, and reconcilers.

And so, the radical ethical teachings of Jesus create tension between the present and final stages of the kingdom of God.

The genuine disciple of Jesus lives in this tension by seizing the many opportunities to do good today. To quote John Wesley, "Do all the good you can. By all the means you can. In all the ways you can. In all the places you can. At all the times you can. To all the people you can. As long as ever you can." Amen.

Eighth Sunday in Ordinary Time

I read about an angry man who stormed into the postmaster's office, waving several pieces of mail. "For weeks I've been pestered with threatening letters," he shouted, "and I want something done about it." "I'm sure we can help," the postmaster calmly replied. "It's against the law to send threats through the mail. Who's sending these threatening letters?" The man snapped, "It's those people in the IRS." The moral of the story: don't mess with the IRS.

The word of God carries us back in our imaginations to the sixth century before Jesus (the 500s) to a prophet who spoke to a people who had lost everything they thought would endure forever: their kingdom—now conquered, their city Jerusalem—now ruined, and their temple—now razed to the ground. And even worse, many of these Hebrews were deported to ancient Babylonia. The prophet asked rhetorically, "Has God completely forgotten us?" But he answered immediately. No. "Can a mother forget her infant? And even if she should, I will never forget you" (Isa 49:14–15).

The author's words challenge us to trust that God is always near us, even when he seems so far away.

Paul, in his letter to the Christian community in Corinth, spoke about his vocation or calling as a servant of Jesus Christ, a steward of the divine mysteries. Paul possessed the qualities of an effective disciple, qualities that ought to be ours as well. They included an awareness of God's presence in his life and in the lives of others, empathy especially for the needy, courage, loyalty to the tradition handed down, a sense of mission, and an ability to verbalize the content of faith in Jesus Christ (1 Cor 4:1–5).

Paul was a grace to others by being grace himself. And we also can be a grace to one another by being grace ourselves.

Paul then reminded the Corinthians that God's judgment alone mattered and challenged us to be faithful to our baptismal calling. Do not judge other people negatively, Paul urged. Why? Because God ultimately will bring to light our motives for doing or not doing the right thing.

In the Gospel according to Matthew, the author's words challenge us not to worry and fret about so many things (Mt 6:24–34). But we all worry, don't we? We worry about many things, including our health, our money, our children, our parents, our retirement pensions, and so forth.

Take the "worry test." Ask yourself, What keeps me awake at night? The answer may tell you where your heart is.

How many remember the 1990s book *Don't Sweat the Small Stuff: And It's All Small Stuff?*

The letter of Peter urges us to cast all our worries on God because he cares for us. Good Pope John XXIII had the right attitude. I suppose that's why he's a saint. When Pope John convened the Second Vatican Council in 1962, all kinds of controversies swirled around the church. One evening while his secretary was fretting about these disagreements, Pope John suddenly announced he was going to bed. The bewildered secretary asked, "How can you sleep at night?" Pope John calmly responded that he was putting all his worries in the hands of God. "God's up all night," he noted. "And besides, it's his church, not mine." That's a good attitude to have.

Discipleship, the gospel writer continued, requires a single, wholehearted commitment to God. We can't divide our loyalty between God and mammon, between God and the greedy quest for wealth, power, or fame. Seek first the kingdom of God. First things first. Focus first on our relationship with God and one another. And do our best every day, as if it were our only one.

On Ash Wednesday, we will have our foreheads smudged with ashes and begin the Lenten season once more. It's a time to consider our priorities in life again.

Leo Tolstoy, the nineteenth-century Russian author, can be a good introduction to priorities. Many of us probably had to read his novels *Anna Karenina* and *War and Peace*. But Tolstoy also wrote shorter, profoundly religious novels. In some ways, they are like religious parables—good spiritual reading for Lent.

A Confession, for example, describes Tolstoy's own search for meaning and purpose. He discovered that the simple farm people of Russia found the answer to this question of purpose through their lively Christian faith, their relationship with God.

Perhaps Tolstoy's masterpiece was the seventy-five-page novel *The Death of Ivan Ilyich*. The story is simple. A man on his deathbed realizes he has wasted his life by living badly, and he's terrified of his fast-approaching death. Tolstoy focuses our attention on Ilyich's life, illness, and spiritual crisis.

Most of the characters imagine what Ilyich's death means for their own lives and think of how grateful they are that it's Ilyich and not they who must die. Ilyich's best friend competes with Ilyich's widow in seeing who can pretend to be more devastated. The mixture of selfishness and disingenuousness is obvious.

Ilyich, in exchange for luxury and status, has sacrificed his authenticity and integrity. The result is a spiritual barrenness that leaves him ill equipped to deal with the specter of death. Ilyich always presumed that death was something for other people. Now he realizes its inescapability. He faces a mortality he never acknowledged.

Avoiding thoughts about death in favor of thoughts about superficialities isn't a flaw reserved for nineteenth-century Russians. It's the story of everyone.

Ilyich's last days are worsened by his realization that he has squandered his short time on earth with shallow trivialities. The servant who attends to him at his deathbed is everything Ilyich is not: humble, poor, devout, and selfless. Ilyich manages to learn the purpose of life from the servant just before his last breath.

Tolstoy suddenly bathes Ilyich in light but leaves the reader in suspense about Ilyich's salvation or damnation. This novel can be powerful Lenten spiritual reading, because Lent is about asking who and what our most important priorities are. We follow Jesus, who went out into the wilderness for forty days to ask the same questions.

The twentieth-century writer Frederick Buechner asked his readers to consider their priorities. Buechner gave us an examination of conscience in these questions:

> If you had only one last message to leave to the handful of people who are most important to you, what would it be in twenty-five words or less? Of all the things you have done in your life, which is the one you would most like to undo? Which is the one that makes you happiest to remember? If this were the last day of your life, what would you do with it? To try to answer questions like these is to begin to hear something not only of who you are but of the way you are becoming and what you are failing to become.

It can be a pretty depressing business, Buechner noted. "But if sackcloth and ashes are at the start of it, something like Easter may be at the end."

As we begin the Lenten season again, let us ask God for the grace to get our priorities straight and pursue them single-mindedly.

FIRST SUNDAY OF LENT

I read about a husband and wife who had a turbulent fifty-year marriage. Their arguments could be heard all over the neighborhood. The husband would shout, "When I die, I will dig my way out of the grave and haunt you for the rest of your life!" Even the neighbors feared him.

After the husband died, the wife's neighbors asked, "Aren't you afraid that he may be able to dig his way out of the grave?" The wife calmly replied, "Let him dig. I had him buried upside down. And I know he won't ask for directions."

We have begun our Lenten journey from ashes to Easter. Last Wednesday we had our foreheads smudged with ashes and heard the prayer "Remember, you are dust and to dust you will return." Dust represents the human condition. It symbolizes how transitory and fragile human life is: here today, gone tomorrow.

Lent is a forty-day retreat. It's a time to ask again, Who and what are our most important priorities in life? Yes, it's a time to follow Jesus into the wilderness and into the desert—not only to confront the demons or addictions within us but also to replenish ourselves with the gifts of the Spirit (for example, wisdom, good judgment, and courage). Lent is a time to recall how the Jews of old saw the desert. It was not only an abode of wild beasts and demons but also a place where a person encountered God and where God encountered the person.

So what are we bringing into the wilderness where God will encounter us and we will encounter God? Maybe you're feeling an emptiness, a dissatisfaction. Things are going okay, but you're starting to wonder, *Is this what it's all about?* You're building an impressive résumé, but what does it all mean in the end? Let this be the season to focus on doing the right thing. To quote Shakespeare in *Hamlet*, "To thine own self be true."

Maybe you find yourself facing new challenges and problems you may not have expected—making the family income stretch a little more, living with a serious illness, needing to support a son or daughter through an especially difficult time.

Or maybe you're encountering a new development in life: a wedding, the birth of a child, or an anxious first year of college away from home.

Or maybe you're confronting the "tempter." You must make some tough life-changing decisions. Listen to Jesus's response to his tempter— God instead of bread, service instead of a self-centered life, humility and generosity instead of celebrity.

As you struggle to find your way through a wilderness of doubts, challenges, changes, and decisions, remember that Jesus also trekked through the wilderness. So during this Lent, stop and ask for directions in the solitude of prayer and conversation with those you love and who love you. Lent is a time to stop, to look at our options, to ask, Who am I? Where am I going, and what's my true purpose in life? It's a time to reflect on what we want our lives to be and why God gave us life in the first place.

During these forty days of Lent, the Spirit leads us to rediscover the presence of God in our lives, to walk with Jesus as our traveling companion through our own wilderness, and to let his Spirit of compassion and his light of wisdom subdue the "tempter" as we strive to be a grace to others by being grace ourselves. Lent challenges us to fix our eyes on the things that truly matter, to have a change of heart, and to live in a better relationship with God and one another.

The word of God carries us back to three characters: a man, a woman, and a snake. The story explains how evil entered the world. In the beginning, the book of Genesis said, God fashioned a magnificent universe and created man and woman to enjoy it. They walked with God; they had friendship with God and friendship with one another.

It's a symbolic story. There's the tree of life, like in so many ancient Near East stories. But there's another tree, the one that gave knowledge of good and evil, a tree symbolizing divine status. Enter the snake. The snake was cunning. It slithered through the grass and talked and laid low the unwary. It set people against one another and against God. The man and woman wanted divine status, to be self-sufficient, so they ate the "forbidden fruit." They suddenly were a laughingstock—naked. They lost their friendship with God and fell from grace. Evil intruded into their lives. And ever since, although we are intrinsically good, left to our own devices, we tend to choose evil over good. How else can we explain the appalling violence in century after century (Gn 2:7–9; 3:1–7)?

Ever since the fall from grace, human beings have desperately cried out for God's healing power. And that is why God became one of us in Jesus of Nazareth—so we could have God's friendship again.

The author's words may be asking us whether we see God as our friend, as our walking companion as we face doubts, challenges, and decisions.

Paul, in his letter to the Christian community at Rome, said very simply that, just as we fell from God's grace or friendship through the first Adam, so now through the second Adam, the crucified and risen Christ, we have God's grace or friendship again (Rom 5:12–19).

Paul's words may be asking us whether we are living a godlike life, a life of virtue as a friend of God should.

In the Gospel according to Matthew, Jesus was tempted in the wilderness as the ancient Hebrews were tested in the wilderness centuries before. Would Jesus simply satisfy his physical hunger at the expense of his mission or purpose in life? No. His food was to do the will of his heavenly Father. Or would Jesus simply work signs and wonders so people would puff up his ego? No. Jesus refused to play superman to suit his fancy or whim. Or would Jesus seek political power so people would kowtow to him? No. Jesus refused to worship anyone, to adore anything except God alone. Jesus won't make a god out of material goods, celebrity status, or political power. No. He will seek only to do the will of his heavenly Father (Mt 4:1–11).

Jesus may be asking whether we are pursuing wealth, power, celebrity, or whatever at the expense of what truly matters—our relationships with God and one another.

Lent tells us it's time to ask God for the grace to get our priorities straight. It's a time for prayer, a time to do without unnecessary things so the needy can have necessary things, a time to reach out with a helping hand to others, whether through volunteer service, charitable giving, or whatever. For hundreds of years, Lent has focused on these three disciplines: prayer, fasting, and almsgiving. Rediscover and retreat yourself to these age-old disciplines again this Lent.

SECOND SUNDAY OF LENT

A few of you may be aware that I'm not known for my culinary skills. Many years ago, I decided to prepare a pasta dinner on a wintry evening for a few Franciscan friars. But I insisted on one condition. If the spaghetti wasn't up to snuff, they wouldn't say a word. They were simply to get up from the table, and we'd eat at a local restaurant. When I brought the food into the dining room, they already had their overcoats on. So much for my cooking.

Some of you have probably heard the following advice from a wise old man. "When I was young, my prayer was, 'Lord, give me the energy to change the world.' As I approached middle age and realized my life was half gone, I changed my prayer to, 'Lord, give me the grace to change all I meet.' Now that I am old and my days are numbered, I have begun to see how foolish I have been. My prayer now is, 'Lord, give me the grace to change myself.'"

That is indeed a good Lenten prayer. As we "spring forward," as the cold of winter changes in many parts of the country to the warmth of spring, the Lenten season calls for a similar change within ourselves: letting the coldness of a self-centered life be transformed into a more God-centered, others-centered life of love, forgiveness, compassion, and peacemaking.

Last Sunday we were in the wilderness in the presence of Jesus and the tempter. Evil abounded. This week we're on top of a mountain in the presence of God, Jesus, and his transfiguration. Good abounds more. Lent is a time to affirm our belief in the presence of God in our world, in the good news that Jesus Christ not only overcame evil but also gave us this Lenten time so we would believe more in the power of the good news than in the sadness of the bad news.

The word of God takes us back almost four thousand years to the land we know today as Iraq. Abraham heard the call of God. And because he was an ordinary man with an extraordinary faith, because he trusted completely in God, he set out for an unknown land. Many of us can relate to this. Remember going off to college? Or to a new job? Or to another place? You may have been anxious. I'm sure Abraham was. Yet because Abraham trusted in God's unconditional love, God made a covenant with him and promised him prosperity (Gn 12:1-4).

This God also calls us to be people of faith, to trust him completely as we, like Abraham, journey through happy, disappointing, and uncertain days to our heavenly dwelling place.

In his letter to Timothy, Paul spoke about God's tremendous love for us. God is indeed the tremendous lover, a title of a book. Yes, God is always ready to lift us up. This God became one of us in Jesus of Nazareth so we could become like God. And one day we shall see God as God really is, face-to-face. An awesome vision! (2 Tm 1:8–10).

That is why Paul urged us to live a holy life now—a life in the presence of God and in service to one another.

Many of you know of Mother Teresa of Calcutta, a model of persistence in faith and prayer despite doubts and darkness. She showed that holiness isn't a luxury for the few; it is meant for all. One story I will never forget. A so-called "untouchable" was alone and dying on the sidewalk. The nun went over, put her hands together as if in prayer, and bowed to him with a Hindu greeting: namaste. She saw the image and glory of God underneath this unkempt and emaciated man. And, as the story goes, he looked at her and uttered his dying words. "I lived with animals, and now I die with the angels."

Yes, to see the image of God in people despite a "distressing disguise" is to live a holy life.

In the Gospel according to Matthew, the disciples experienced the transfiguration of Jesus; they saw the unique and awesome presence of God in Jesus (Mt 17:1–9).

As the scriptures describe this, the face of Jesus became as dazzling as the sun, his clothes as "white as light," an allusion to the white tunic on early Christians as they arose from the baptismal waters. The disciples suddenly glimpsed a vision of the "glorious" Jesus beyond the flesh and blood Jesus they knew. They also saw their own future in the transfigured Jesus.

Jesus had to live by faith, completely trusting in his Father's unconditional love for him. That faith made Jesus a transformative person, ushering in the kingdom of God. That faith was tested to the breaking point on the cross. To quote twentieth-century theologian Karl Rahner, "Jesus surrendered himself in his death unconditionally to the absolute mystery that he calls his Father, into whose hands he committed his existence when in the night of his death and God-forsakenness he was deprived of everything that is otherwise regarded as the content of a human existence: life, honor, acceptance and so forth."

Jesus died as he had lived, with faith in his heavenly Father, with hope of life forever. Yes, he died, murmuring, "Father, into your hands I entrust my spirit." And in the mystery of death, God transfigured Jesus into a new kind of spiritual embodiment.

And just as Jesus became a transformative person in ushering in the kingdom of God, so too Jesus calls us, his coworkers, to become transformative people as well. We, as coworkers with God, must do our best to transform unfairness and prejudice into fairness and tolerance; to transform hate into peace, indifference into compassion, sorrow into joy, and despair into hope. Yes, we must work to transform self-centeredness into others-centeredness so we, like the risen Christ, can be transfigured into a new kind of spiritual embodiment.

I close with a few rules for success from a coach who changed a mediocre college football team into a winning team, Notre Dame icon Lou Holtz. He recognized that attitude determines how well one performs any task. Here are a few of his transformative thoughts:

> Focus on your character. Be trustworthy. Behave honorably. When you make a mistake, make amends.

Show people you care. Prove it consistently by praising people's efforts. Show your enthusiasm. Both a great attitude and a bad attitude are contagious.

Surround yourself with people who encourage, not discourage. Set the right example. Your hard work can generate the feeling that everyone is in it together.

Know what you want; set goals at every stage in life. Work hard to achieve them. And when negative thoughts arise, start thinking, "I can." It works a lot better than "I can't."

Let this be our prayer for Lent. Just practicing this prayer will make us transformative persons in the lives of people.

Forgiving those we don't want to forgive;
having compassion;
making peace;
caring for those in need, even though it's inconvenient;
persevering when we are exhausted;
carrying our crosses when we want to run away from them; and
loving when the last thing we want to do is love.

THIRD SUNDAY OF LENT

You may have heard about the teenager who, excited about getting his driver's license, asked his father about a car. The father replied, "Let's talk about it after you bring your grades up, do your chores, and start getting haircuts." Three months later the teenager reported his grades were up and his chores were done well. The father said, "Yes, but you haven't got a haircut." The teenager replied, "Moses had long hair. Samson had long hair. Jesus had long hair. What's the big deal?" The father responded, "You're right. They also walked wherever they went, so why not forget the car and walk?" The teen got a haircut.

We are in the middle of the Lenten season. This is a six-week journey into the paschal mystery, the mystery of dying/rising, his and ours; the mystery of life in and through death. Each Sunday in Lent reflects on life as in a prism. On first Sunday, a hungry Jesus told the tempter what makes for life, not bread alone but every word from God; on last Sunday, the transfiguration, God reveals the divine in the human Jesus, our lives. Next Sunday, light and darkness, the man born blind sees life. On the fifth Sunday, Lazarus is called from death to life. And on Passion/Palm Sunday, life leaps out of death. Yes, life—the gift of God's life, initially ours in baptism, weaves in and out of the Lenten season. And today Jesus is life-giving water for the thirsty woman at the well.

The word of God carries us back in our imaginations to a central moment in the life of the Hebrews, their exodus, freedom, or deliverance from their oppressors. Here they were wandering in the wilderness and complaining. *Where is God now?* they wondered as they faced hunger and thirst. Moses cried out to God for help, and God demonstrated his presence among them. Water suddenly flowed from a rock and quenched their thirst (Ex 17:3–7).

The life-giving waters allude to the waters of our baptism and the promises made to God in baptism. Baptism is a rite of initiation into a global Catholic community. And what is the significance of this rite? Early Christian candidates for baptism were often literally immersed in water. Water could be life giving, or it could be death threatening (a hurricane). And when the candidate stepped into the pool of water and came up out of the pool, in that gesture he or she professed a dying to a self-centered life and rising to an others-centered, God-centered life.

The author's words may be asking us whether we live a God-centered life.

In his letter to the Christian community at Rome, Paul spoke about the saving, healing work of Jesus Christ. Through his horrendous death and glorious resurrection, we have access to God, friendship with God. God's love and life have been poured out into us in the waters of baptism so we can reflect the glory or presence of God in our daily lives (Rom 5:1–2, 5–8).

Paul may wonder whether our attitudes and behaviors do precisely that.

In the Gospel according to John, Jesus asked for water from a woman of questionable character (she had five husbands) and from a despised people (the Samaritans), only to engage her in a conversation about thirst. Jesus revealed who he was. He was a prophet, the Messiah, the source who gifts us with eternal life, living water who can satisfy our quest for meaning in life. In faith, this woman discovered new purpose through her encounter with Jesus and heralded the good news of Jesus to her townsfolk (Jn 4:5–42).

We all thirst like Jesus and the woman at the well, don't we? But what are we thirsty for? What turns us on? Some simply thirst for a decent livelihood. Others thirst for health, wealth, pleasure, power, and fame. Still others, like the Samaritan woman, thirst for purpose in life.

Today I would like to reflect on a modern icon who thirsted for God, Therese of Lisieux. She asked God to transform her into his image, and that's precisely what God did.

Fr. Kevin E. Mackin, OFM

Therese lived and died in the late nineteenth century in the obscurity of a Carmelite cloister in Normandy, France. We know about her through her remarkable autobiography, *The Story of a Soul*, which documents her search for God and made her a guru in Catholic spirituality.

Therese's life was quite ordinary. A happy childhood suddenly changed to struggles with depression at the death of her mother when she was only four. At fifteen, she had the moxie to ask Pope Leo XIII to let her enter the cloister. With persistence, she did, and for the next nine years she pursued a spiritual pathway she came to call the "little way." She died at twenty-four, still struggling with doubts about God and yet holding onto a crucifix as she spoke her dying words—"My God, I love You."

The words of the father in Jesus's healing of the boy in Mark's gospel could have been hers and perhaps ours sometimes. "I do believe; help my unbelief."

So, what is this "little way" anyone can supposedly follow? For me, it's made up of three ingredients. First, Therese realized her own insignificance. Think about it. There are some seven billion people on this planet—perhaps billions before and perhaps billions after. And some say there are at least ten trillion planets in our galaxy alone and at least two hundred billion galaxies out there. Wow! We really are insignificant. And yet God gave us significance. God, who is love, created us out of love from nothingness so he could be one with us. Therese personified humility. Her response was always gratitude to God that she even existed.

Second, Therese recognized that God loved her unconditionally. That's why she had a childlike trust and lived a childlike life, completely dependent on the love of her Father in heaven and always receptive to whatever gifts God bestowed on her.

Finally, because God loved her unconditionally, Therese loved God unconditionally, even though throughout her life she often wondered where God was. She believed despite her unbelief. Therese did small things extraordinarily well out of love for God. She accepted the will of God as expressed in the daily routine of cloistered life. In every situation, she willed the good of others, no matter how annoying or mean spirited they seemed to her.

Therese of Lisieux wasn't simply content with a safe place in heaven.

She wanted to spend heaven doing good on earth. And that is why so many people honor her today. Her "little way" quenched her thirst for God as Jesus quenched the thirst of the Samaritan at the well.

Therese's "little way" can be a spiritual guide for us—gratitude to God, a childlike trust in a God who loves us unconditionally, and doing ordinary things extraordinarily well out of love for God.

During these Lenten days, I invite all of us to renew ourselves spiritually and rededicate ourselves in regular prayer to God and in generous service to one another. Then when we renew our baptismal promises at Easter, we will reexperience the presence of God more deeply.

FOURTH SUNDAY OF LENT

You may have heard about the man who went to his doctor with concerns about his health and appearance. "I feel terrible," the patient said. "When I look in the mirror, I see a balding head, sagging jowls, a potbelly, crooked teeth, bloodshot eyes ... I'm a mess! I desperately need good news to boost my self-image." The physician responded, "Well, the good news is, you have perfect eyesight."

I recently rediscovered an ad for a Lenten skin treatment. For the lips, use the ointment of silence—it's especially good for lips chapped with backbiting, coarse language, and untruths. For better hands, employ generosity. It contains a base of love with essences of kindness and thoughtfulness. For clear eyes, use liturgy. It helps you see God, nourishes a desire to practice virtue, and is a preservative for eternal life. And for cleansing lotion, apply reconciliation. It relieves tension, begets grace, and restores hope. Take the full treatment; you'll look fabulous spiritually.

Today's word of God challenges us to always look beyond appearances and with the gift of faith to discover three realities: Jesus as the light who illumines the purpose of life; ourselves as a light to others in our attitude and behavior; and our fellow human beings as bearers of the light or presence of God, no matter how hidden that presence may be.

The word of God takes us back over three thousand years. King Saul made a mess of things, perhaps like some political dictators today. God inspired the prophet Samuel to look for another king in a sheepherder's family of eight brothers. At first, David was overlooked. He was the youngest, the most unlikely choice. Think of great leaders in our country and how unlikely they appeared to many people. George Washington, for example, often looked downright unfriendly with his wooden false teeth. Abraham Lincoln had a homely face. FDR was wheelchair bound. Yet, despite appearances, they became great presidents.

The unlikely David became king of ancient Israel. God saw in David the incredible potential for leadership others didn't see (1 Sm 16:1, 6–7, 10–13).

The word challenges us not to stereotype people—to write them off, so to speak—but rather to look underneath and beyond appearances to the incredible potential for good people have and to try to bring out their best qualities by affirming them, not negatively criticizing them.

In his letter to the Christian community in Ephesus in Turkey, Paul reflected on light and darkness. Light can transform a cold night into a warm day. Light enables us to study, to discover, and to behold the wonders of God's universe. In short, light warms, nurtures, sustains, reveals and cheers. Paul urged us to live as children of light, pleasing God in our attitude and behavior (Eph 5:8–14). Jesus is indeed our light.

Blessed John Henry Newman captured Jesus as light in a wonderful poem.

> Lead, Kindly Light, amidst th'encircling gloom,
> Lead Thou me on!
> The night is dark, and I am far from home,
> Lead Thou me on! …
> Lead me home in childlike faith,
> Home to my God.

So often, people walk in darkness about the purpose of their lives and forget that Jesus is the light who illumines our pathway into eternal life. We too are called to be light to people, to let our life shine forth with virtues such as honesty, integrity, responsibility, courage, perseverance, compassion, and faith in God.

In the Gospel according to John, Jesus cured a blind man. He opened the eyes of this man so he could see reality. But notice how blind some of the characters in this story were. The Pharisees, for example, were blinded by protocol—how dare Jesus heal on the Sabbath! They also were blinded to the power of God working outside their own religious structures. The parents were also blinded by fear and refused to stand up for what they knew was true (Jn 9:1–41).

The gospel author's words challenge us to see Jesus through the lens of faith as the light who illumines the purpose of life.

I think of a twentieth-century monk, Thomas Merton, OCSO, who wrote about his own search for light in his best-selling autobiography, *The Seven Storey Mountain*, which chronicles his conversion from a carefree university lifestyle to a religious life with the Trappist monks at the Abbey of Gethsemani in Kentucky.

Merton, orphaned at sixteen, lived a sort of vagabond youth. At Cambridge University, he engaged in reckless drinking and carousing, and then moved to New York and enrolled at Columbia University. There he delighted his classmates with his wit and charm, became the editor of the student literary publication, and befriended Robert Lax.

Merton's chance encounter with a classic philosophical book about the Christian understanding of God changed his life. He went with Lax to St. Bonaventure University in upstate New York, where he became instructor of English. (Olean, New York, isn't the end of the world, but you can see it from Olean.)

Merton eventually applied to join the Franciscan friars but was rejected. Imagine that: Merton rejected, and Mackin accepted.

But a friend advised Merton about the Trappists, and off he went to Kentucky. He was based there for the remaining twenty-seven years of his life as a monk, priest, author, and spiritual guru. The abbey's mantra was *ora et labora* (pray and work). Merton wrote dozens of books and hundreds of poems and articles, and he corresponded with religious thinkers and cultural icons all over the world.

He gradually moved from the insular world of the abbey to the wider world of politics and religion, in correspondence with political movers and shakers and people of different faiths or no faith. All of us, Merton argued, are children of God. Faithful to his Catholic tradition, Merton was always open to the truth in other religious traditions, especially Eastern religions. He died tragically in Thailand at age fifty-three.

Throughout his Trappist life, Merton tried to live a life of prayer or intimacy with God through the chanting of the psalms during the day, the daily Eucharist, and such religious practices as the stations of the cross and the mysteries of the rosary. Above all, Merton sought solitude and contemplation, that inner center within himself where he could feel God's love sustaining him. That's why he sought Buddhist techniques, for example, to help find that inner stillness.

In his work *Seeds of Contemplation*, Merton noted that noise more than anything else sabotages contemplation and blocks out the voice of God within us. Merton asked for the grace—and it indeed is a grace—to clear his mind of earthly concerns so that in solitude he could move beyond thoughts and words into a felt awareness of the presence of God within himself. There he would sit still and listen to God's voice.

Yes, he sought to find his true self in God through God abiding in him and he in God. Moreover, Merton sensed the oneness of God all about him—in all creatures and all creation. All were holy. The invisible light of God in all creatures simply must be made visible.

Our Lenten task, Merton might say, is to let the image of God become manifest in who we are so we become the very likeness of God.

FIFTH SUNDAY OF LENT

You may have heard about the fire-and-brimstone preacher who thundered from the pulpit, "Everyone in this parish is going to die." A man in the first pew burst out laughing. Annoyed, the preacher roared louder. "I said everyone in this parish is going to die." Again, the man burst out laughing. The preacher, really irritated, shouted, "What's so funny about that?" The man in the pew answered, "I don't belong to this parish." Was he in for a surprise!

In the lobby of a chapel at Oxford University, there's a statue of Lazarus bound from head to foot. Jesus, you remember, cried out, "Untie him and let him go." That image symbolizes what every church should be about: untying people from the many things that hold them back from their relationship with God. A powerful prayer whenever we enter a church is, "Untie me from attitudes and behaviors that prevent me from becoming my true self: the likeness of God."

The word of God carries us back to the sixth century before Jesus. The Hebrews were despondent. The Babylonians had conquered them, demolished the temple in Jerusalem, and deported many Hebrews to Babylonia. But here Ezekiel proclaimed that God would breathe his spirit into the "bones" of the demoralized Hebrews. They would become new creatures. The image is graphic. The dead bones would knit together, flesh would cover them, and the spirit of God would breathe new life into them (Eze 37:12–14).

The author may have been challenging us to live as new creatures, called to become like God in our attitudes and behaviors.

In his letter to the Christian community at Rome, Paul declared that the spirit of God, who raised Jesus from the dead, dwells within us. That spirit can energize us so we will manifest the fruit of the spirit: love, joy, peace, patience, kindness, generosity, faithfulness, gentleness, and self-control (Rom 8:8–11).

Paul may be asking us to pray that the spirit of God would transform us into "living temples or shrines of God" in our everyday lives.

In the Gospel according to John, Jesus cried out, "Lazarus, come out of the tomb!" And out came Lazarus, bound with burial wrappings (Jn 11:1–45).

Two things always puzzled me about this passage. If Jesus really loved Lazarus, why didn't he rush to Lazarus when he first heard the news of his illness? Instead, Jesus stayed where he was for two more days. But in fact, this timing emphasized the raising of Lazarus as a threshold sign in our own salvation history.

Second, "Jesus wept." These were probably tears of friendship. Jesus lost a friend and didn't have a chance to say goodbye. But then Jesus gave Lazarus a second chance; he brought Lazarus back to physical life. I always wondered, *Did Lazarus ever describe to his sisters what he experienced when he was dead for four days?* After all, people have described their near-death experiences. And also, did this "second chance" change Lazarus dramatically?

In some ways, we are like Lazarus. We have been given many second chances, so to speak. But are we doing anything differently with these second chances?

Today I would like to reflect on life and grieving—life for Lazarus and the initial grief of his sisters, Martha and Mary.

Nobel Prize-winning playwright Eugene O'Neill, who wrote *Long Day's Journey into Night*, also wrote the play *Lazarus Laughed*. In the play, people gathered at Lazarus's home. They came to mourn. But now, Lazarus was raised from the dead, and the grieving was transformed into rejoicing. Lazarus's father proposed a toast. "To my son, Lazarus, whom a blessed miracle has brought back from death."

Lazarus interrupted, "No! There is no death." And the folks holding their wine goblets echoed as a question, "There's no death?" And Lazarus laughed and said happily, "There is only life. I heard the heart of Jesus laughing in my own heart. 'There is only eternal life,' it said. 'Laugh, laugh with me. Fear is no more.' Fear not, for the Lord is with you. Fear not, for the Lord is telling you, 'If anyone believes in me, even though they die, they will live, and whoever lives and believes in me will never die.'"

There it is, folks. Jesus conquered death. Life leaped out of death. Nothing will ever separate us from the love of God, to paraphrase Paul's words to the Romans. Yes, we are alive with the life of God. We are shrines of the Spirit, whose hidden power equips us with his gifts so we can become our true selves in the likeness of God. These are gifts of wisdom to focus on what truly matters; understanding and knowledge to enter deeply into the mysteries of God; counsel to make good moral decisions; fortitude to stand up for what is right; piety to give God praise and worship; and fear of the Lord, a healthy concern never to lose that relationship with God.

Yes, there's eternal life. But how can we reconcile eternal life with earthly grief?

C. S. Lewis wrote a book, *The Problem of Pain*, that discusses theoretically the problem of evil. It's an eternal question highlighted in the biblical book of Job. If God is good, why does he let evil happen? God never answers Job's question. Why do the good suffer and the wicked prosper? There's only silence.

C. S. Lewis wrote another book, *A Grief Observed*, that explores the process of grieving in the dying and death of his wife only three years after their wedding. One of the last things his wife said was, "I am at peace with God."

Lewis detailed his thoughts about life without his wife and his anger and bewilderment at God. He felt a sense of distance from God, a deadening silence, what the sixteenth century Carmelite John of the Cross called the "dark night of the soul."

Lewis had doubts. He asked, "Is this what God is really like?" But gradually some of the clouds of grief began to lift with the passage of time. Anger and doubt gave way to acceptance and peace and faith. Lewis described this feeling like the breaking through of the sun after an overcast morning.

In some ways, Lewis wrote, God had to shatter his youthful faith, which was like a "house of cards" so he could fashion an adult faith. Lewis came to realize that it's healthy to think about mortality from time to time. It puts things in perspective and reminds us of what truly matters. It compels us to reorder our priorities, to focus on our deeply held values, and to celebrate the joy and purpose of the gift of life.

Life is a pilgrimage, a journey, a passage. We must let go of the past to go forward, and to let go means to die a little. Yes, we let go, and eventually we let go of our earthly lives so we can become transfigured, like Jesus Christ before us, into a new kind of spiritual embodiment. St. Paul wonderfully highlighted the prophet Isaiah's realization: "What eye has not seen, and ear has not heard, and what has not entered the human heart, what God has prepared for those who love him." (1Co 2:9)

We come back to Jesus, Lazarus, and ourselves. We might shout to Jesus in light of today's gospel, "Untie me from the attitudes and behaviors that prevent me from becoming my true self: the likeness of God."

Life and death—we are forever changing, and everything around us is changing. But change involves loss, and loss involves grief, and grief involves pain.

And yet our faith proclaims that life leaps out of death. In the agony of our Good Fridays is the ecstasy of Easter.

Palm Sunday of the Passion of the Lord

On Ash Wednesday, our global Catholic community invited us to treat ourselves to those age-old exercises of prayer ("heart-to-heart" conversation with God), fasting (doing without, for example, negative attitudes and behaviors that can jeopardize our relationship with God and one another), and almsgiving (generously sharing what we have) so we can deepen our friendship with God and our fellow human beings. I hope these exercises have reinvigorated us and deepened our faith in God.

Today, Palm Sunday, we begin Holy Week, the chief week of the liturgical year. We focus on the paschal mystery (the dying and rising of Jesus Christ). We contemplate the journey of Jesus from this earthly life through the mystery of death into a transfigured heavenly life.

The word *paschal* comes from the Hebrew *pesach* or the "passing" of the angel of death over the homes of the Hebrews in ancient Egypt centuries ago (a "passing over" that spared their firstborn child from death). In a larger sense, the Passover refers to the exodus or liberation of the Hebrews from their oppressors. Every year the Jewish community reexperiences this liberation in what is called a seder service.

I came across a story that highlights for me the significance of our Holy Week. A high school teacher in an Iowa farm community gave her students an unusual assignment. She asked the students to bring to class a plastic bag and a sack of potatoes.

In class, she asked each student to take a potato for every person the student had refused to forgive or treated badly. The student was to write the name of the person and the date on the potato and put the potato in a plastic bag. The teacher then told the students to carry their bags of potatoes with them for the day—putting the bag of potatoes next to their desks when they did their homework, next to their chairs at the dinner table, and next to their beds that night. They also needed to lug them back to school the next day.

As you can imagine, carrying around that sack of potatoes became an embarrassing affair. The students definitely were happy to drop their sacks off the following day in school.

But the exercise taught a valuable lesson about the time and energy we waste lugging our anger and guilt around. Too often, we think of forgiveness as a gift to another person, but it is clearly a gift to ourselves as well. We must throw away our anger about the way some people may have mistreated us, and we must throw away our guilt about the way we may have mistreated other people.

Forgiveness and reconciliation are what Holy Week is all about.

On this day, Palm Sunday, we reflect on a paradox: the triumphal entry of Jesus into Jerusalem (in the procession with palms) and the gospel proclamation of the passion and death of Jesus. Triumph and tragedy. Yes, in the tragedy of Good Friday, there is the triumph of

Easter; in and through the death of Jesus, there is resurrection. Life has many paradoxes, doesn't it?

The word of God from Isaiah is a poem about a "servant" who suffers; Paul's letter to the Christian community at Philippi quotes an early Christian hymn about God, who became one of us so we could become one with God; and the gospel proclaims the passion and death of Jesus (Isa 50:4–7; Phil 2:6–11; Mt 26:14–27; 27:11–54).

Thursday, Friday, and Saturday are the triduum or "three days" from the Latin *tres* and *dies*. On Thursday we will commemorate the Lord's Supper. There are the washing of feet (a symbol of service) and then a sacrificial meal, where Jesus gave himself to us in the signs of bread and wine. The following words of Jesus capture the significance of this sacrificial meal: "This is my body; this is my blood." "Take and eat; take and drink." "Do this in memory of me."

On Good Friday, we meditate on the passion and death of Jesus—the garden of Gethsemane, the trial, the crucifixion, the burial, the veneration of the cross—and then we have a simple communion service.

At the Easter vigil, we reflect on the passage of Jesus from this earthly life through death into a transfigured heavenly life; the resurrection of Jesus is a pledge of our own liberation from death or nothingness into a transfigured heavenly life.

The vigil includes fire (a symbol of Jesus as the light who illuminates the darkness around us), the proclamation of the story of our salvation in the scriptures, the renewal of our baptismal promises, and the Eucharistic or thanksgiving prayer.

Easter proclaims that Jesus is risen—alive among us and especially in the sacramental life of our Catholic community.

This is indeed the chief week of the Catholic liturgical year. I pray that your participation in these services will inspire you to seek ever more enthusiastically the God who became flesh in Jesus of Nazareth, who by his dying and rising opened to us a transfigured life beyond earthly life. By the power of the Spirit, he is alive among us, especially in the sacramental life of the global Catholic community.

May the Lord bless you!

Easter Sunday of the Resurrection of the Lord

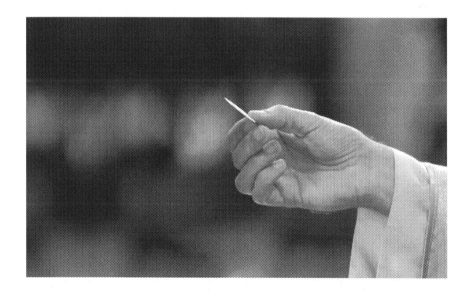

Happy Easter! *Felices Pascuas! Joyeuses Paques! Buona Pasqua! Frohe Ostern!* Jesus Christ lives. And because Christ lives forever, we also live forever. That is the Easter message.

You may have heard about the minister, priest, and rabbi who were kibitzing about death and dying. One of them asked, "When people gather to mourn your death, what would you like them to say?" The minister said, "I would like them to say I was a good family man, a deeply spiritual and caring pastor." The priest replied, "I would like the parishioners to say that I was a good preacher, a prayerful celebrant and a compassionate counselor." The rabbi paused and then said, "I'd like them to say, 'Look, he's moving!'"

Seriously, here's a true story about a man's reaction to his own obituary. A newspaper mistakenly ran his obituary instead of his dead brother's, and what he read shocked him. The newspaper reported the passing of a great industrialist who had amassed a fortune from manufacturing weapons of huge destruction in those days—dynamite. His reputation as a heartless employer and ruthless businessman was also chronicled.

The man was stunned. This wasn't how he wanted to be remembered. From that moment on, he devoted himself to philanthropy, justice, and peace. Today, he is remembered as the founder of the Nobel Prizes. Alfred Nobel said, "Everyone ought to have the chance to correct his or her epitaph in midstream and write a new one."

And so today, in light of Easter, we might ask, "How do we want to be remembered? As someone who made a difference for the better in the lives of some people?" The choice is ours.

The word *Easter* comes from "Eastre," the name of a Saxon goddess of the dawn or spring. Easter symbolizes life.

A popular symbol is the Easter egg. And just as the chick breaks out of the egg at birth, so too we believe that, in the mystery of death, we will break out of this earthly "skin" of ours, so to speak, into a new life. Why do we believe this? Because Jesus, once crucified and dead, is alive. His resurrection is the pledge of our own. The living Christ anticipates what we will become. In the meantime, we must live lives worthy of our baptismal calling as sons and daughters of God our Father.

Easter is about the dawn, daybreak, and beginning again. Jesus's resurrection is a new day for all of us. Every morning we have another chance. Perhaps when we went to bed the night before, we carried baggage—things undone or put off, bad things said and done, good things unsaid and not done. In the morning, all is possibility; all is opportunity. We begin again.

Who among us is content with who we are? Who doesn't want to be more loving, more generous, more compassionate, more helpful? Who wouldn't want the courage to act on our convictions as opposed to our fears? Who among us doesn't know of a heart to heal, a broken relationship to mend, or a lost soul to find?

This Easter God wakes us up again. Let this be the day to start again, to repair the broken, and to rediscover God's extraordinary grace transforming our ordinary lives into the likeness of God.

In the word of God today, Peter proclaimed the *kerygma*, the good news. Peter spoke about all that God has done for us through Jesus of Nazareth (Acts 10:34, 37–43).

Jesus was baptized by John, anointed with the Spirit, and went about the countryside of Judea and Galilee, working signs and wonders, and proclaiming that the kingdom of God was beginning to break into our lives. Eventually Jesus was crucified, but then he burst forth out of the tomb and was lifted to his heavenly Father so he could draw all of us to himself into a new, transfigured heavenly life.

Yes, Jesus is alive, and because he lives, we also live. He is indeed, Peter shouted, a God of mercy and forgiveness. And that's why Pope Francis emphasizes that the church is a field hospital, here to heal wounds.

In his letter to the Christian community in Colossae, Turkey, Paul challenged us to seek God in our everyday lives so we might be with him in glory at the end-time (Col 3:1–4).

In the Gospel according to John, we hear the story of the resurrection of Jesus. Mary Magdalene came to the tomb to find it empty; she summoned Peter and John. The disciples discovered that Jesus wasn't among the dead. He is risen; he is alive. He has passed through the mystery of death into a new, transfigured heavenly reality (Jn 20:1–9).

This heavenly reality is ours as well. That is the Easter message!

The risen Jesus wasn't a spirit or ghost. Nor was he simply resuscitated, or the disciples would have recognized him immediately.

Jesus said, "I live and because I live, we also live." How is that? Born in the flesh, we are reborn in the spirit. In the rite of baptism, the Spirit of God is poured out on us, and a new life is ours. The triune God lives within us, and we live within the triune God.

As we grow in faith, the bishop anoints our forehead with oil in the sign of the cross—and in that gesture God pours out more fully the gifts of the Spirit so we might show forth the fruit of the Spirit in our daily lives: love, joy, peace, patience, kindness, generosity, faithfulness, gentleness, and self-control.

In this Eucharist, the living Christ truly presences himself to us sacramentally and mystically in the signs of bread and wine, and he becomes one with us in communion so we can continue his saving ministry through our hands, feet, voices, and eyes. And if we should stumble on our journey, the living Christ lifts us up in the rite of penance, where we celebrate God's mercy.

Yes, through sacramental encounters with God, we experience the living Christ. In the exchange of wedding promises, God strengthens the love between husband and wife. In the anointing of the sick, God heals our wounds. All the sacraments are indeed signs of God's care for us as we journey to our heavenly dwelling place.

Eternal life in relationship with God and one another—that is our ultimate purpose. In the mystery of our own dying, we believe we will make an evolutionary leap into a new reality, as Jesus already has.

Ours is indeed a faith in a fresh start. Easter is about getting our priorities straight. First things first. Easter is about asking, How can we be more loving, more generous, more compassionate, more helpful? Easter is about seeking a heart to heal, a relationship to mend, a and lost soul to find.

It's a new dawn, a new day, a fresh start.

SECOND SUNDAY OF EASTER

Sometimes in our desire to be profound, we miss the obvious. I think, for example, of an early draft of *The Hound of the Baskervilles*, in which author Arthur Conan Doyle had Sherlock Holmes and Dr. Watson camping out on the Dartmoor. In the middle of the night, Holmes woke up, shook Watson, and said, "Look at the sky, Watson. What do you see?"

Watson replied, "I see stars, millions and millions of stars."

"And what does that tell you?"

Watson paused, then replied, "Astronomically, it tells me there are billions of galaxies and countless planets in them. Horologically, it tells me it's 3 a.m. Theologically, it tells me the universe is charged with the grandeur of God." Holmes was silent. Watson finally asked, "Holmes, what does this magnificent night tell you?"

The detective simply snapped, "Watson, you idiot, it tells me someone stole our tent."

Yes, sometimes in our desire to be profound about the meaning of the Easter season, we miss the obvious. The Easter message is simple. Jesus Christ is risen. He lives. And because he lives, we live forever.

The word of God today carries us back to the beginnings of Christianity, to a particular community that shared what they had. This example should inspire us to create a better sense of community or family—gathering weekly in liturgy to hear God's word and celebrate Christ's presence, studying the Bible more deeply, and generously sharing what we have (Acts 2:42–47).

The letter attributed to Peter speaks about our new birth in the life-giving waters of baptism. God gifted us, the author writes, with an imperishable, heavenly inheritance. And our faith will empower us to overcome hardships and attain our goal of salvation and eternal life with God (1 Pt 1:3–9).

The author may be asking whether we live in accord with that ultimate purpose.

In the Gospel according to John, we find a post-resurrection appearance of Jesus to the disciples in a Jerusalem house. Jesus wasn't simply a spirit or ghost; nor was he simply resuscitated. The resurrected Jesus was the same person. But Jesus's earthly body had been transfigured into a new kind of spiritual embodiment. Christ passed through a sealed tomb and closed doors, appeared, and then disappeared; he wasn't recognizable, and then he was. And in this house, the risen Christ conferred on the excited disciples the power and energy of the Spirit so they and their successors could continue the saving ministry of Jesus in Jerusalem and beyond (Jn 20:19–31). But the skeptical or doubting Thomas wasn't there. Thomas may have been like people today who question whether there's a God.

Perhaps they should recall Blaise Pascal's wager or bet, which goes like this: One doesn't know whether God exists. Not believing in God is bad for one's eternal soul if God does exist. Believing in God is of no consequence if God doesn't exist; therefore, it is in one's interest to believe in God. Think about it.

Thomas here seems to have been a realist. "Where's the evidence?" he probably asked. The disciples described the appearance of the risen Christ in detail. But for Thomas, seeing was believing. Besides, if Christ had appeared, Thomas may have wondered why the doors were still locked. Why were they still hiding? Maybe what Thomas lacked wasn't faith in God but faith in his fellow disciples. After all, they hadn't been very reliable in the garden of Gethsemane.

Yes, faith in people can be as tough today as it was then. Why? Because I think many people have marginalized truth. We must recapture the importance of truth in our lives. Jesus Christ is the foundation of truth. He is the way, the truth, and the life.

The risen Christ in his second visit restored Thomas's faith, prompting the cry, "My Lord and My God." Thomas's prayer could have inspired the prayer in the musical *Godspell*. "Lord, I pray: to see you more clearly, love you more dearly, follow you more nearly."

I like to think that Thomas, like the other disciples, strove to be a person of integrity. Integrity is saying what we think and doing what we say, practicing what we preach. It's all about our moral character.

Nicky Gumbel in *The Jesus Lifestyle* emphasizes the importance of integrity with the image of the *Titanic*. When the *Titanic* set sail, it was declared "unsinkable" because it was constructed using new compartmental technology. Tragically, the *Titanic* sank in April 1912. It was thought that several compartments had been ruptured in a collision with an iceberg. However, when the wreck was later found, there was no sign of the long gash. Investigators discovered that damage to one compartment had affected all the rest.

Many people make the "*Titanic* mistake." They think they can divide their lives into compartments and that what they do in one won't affect the rest. The *Titanic* mistake is trying to confine God to a segment of our lives and cutting him off from the rest. For example, this is my church life, where God is involved. This is my work life, where God can't be involved. This is my social life where I don't want God involved.

Perhaps, Gumbel proposes, think of our life as a circle: God at the center, affecting everything in the circle. That is what I would call a life of integrity, a life not divided. Integrity is doing the right thing, even when nobody is watching. It is a lifelong challenge.

So the question is, How can we avoid the *Titanic* mistake and live lives of integrity in our relationships and with our resources?

First, when we make a promise, we should keep it. Honesty, truthfulness, and reliability are the building blocks of integrity. Loving or always wishing the other person good, no matter how much he or she may have mistreated us, is the context for integrity.

Second, twelve out of Jesus's thirty-eight parables are about money or possessions. Billy Graham put it well when he said, "If a person gets their attitude towards money straight, it will help straighten out almost every other area in their life."

Financial resources are basically a tool for doing good. As my father put it, "I never saw a U-Haul following a hearse." The way we use our financial resources can have eternal consequences. Think of Matthew 25: "When I was hungry, you gave me something to eat." It's not enough to do no harm. We must positively do good.

Jesus challenges us not to love money and use people but rather to love people and use money. Focus on God and the things of God. Think of life as a circle, with God at the center.

I close with Gumbel's story about Pompeii, Italy, in AD 79. Among those who fled from the lava erupting from Mount Vesuvius was a woman who sought to save not only her life but also her jewels. With her hands full of jewelry, she was overwhelmed by the rain of ashes from the volcano and died. During modern excavations outside the area of the buried city, her petrified body was unearthed in a sea of jewels.

She lost her life to save her treasure. Materialism consumed her. We can break the power of materialism by sharing what we have generously and cheerfully.

May we always think of life as a circle with God at the center, affecting everything in that circle.

THIRD SUNDAY OF EASTER

The weather is warming up. And I heard a story about two nuns who were shopping at Trader Joe's on a very hot day. As they passed the beer cooler, one said, "Wouldn't a cool beer be a delight?" The second nun answered, "Yes, but I wouldn't feel comfortable buying beer, as the cashier probably would recognize us." The other nun replied, "Don't worry, let me handle this," and she picked up a six-pack.

The cashier appeared a bit surprised as the nuns approached. "We use beer for washing our hair," the nun said.

The cashier put a bag of pretzels with the beer, smiled, and said, "The curlers are on the house." Moral of the story: you can't fool some folks.

The pyramids in Egypt are a wonder of the ancient world. Over two millennia, numerous scientists, tourists, and grave robbers had searched for the burial places of the pharaohs of ancient Egypt. Many gave up, but Howard Carter, a British archaeologist, pressed on. In 1922 he unlocked the world's most exciting archaeological find: a king's embalmed body in a nest of three coffins, the inner one of solid gold. On the king's head was a magnificent golden portrait mask, and numerous pieces of jewelry were on the body and in its wrappings. Other rooms were crammed with statues, a chariot, weapons, chests, vases, jewels, and a throne.

It was the priceless tomb and treasure of King Tutankhamen, who died in the year 1323 BC. King Tut's tomb was discovered because Howard Carter was persistent, because he persevered.

I believe God reveals himself to us if we persevere. Today's word of God, from one viewpoint, is about persistence, about seeking and finding God.

The passage from the Acts of the Apostles is about Peter, who denied he had been with Jesus, denied he was one of his disciples, and even denied he knew Jesus. But Peter suddenly realized what he had done and wept bitterly. He begged for forgiveness. Later Jesus asked Peter three times, "Do you love me?" And three times Peter undid his triple denial, saying, "You know I love you." Peter had fallen badly, but God lifted him up.

Despite our own falls, God continually lifts us up so we can live lives worthy of our baptismal calling as sons and daughters of God our Father. God repeatedly empowers us to persevere in becoming our true selves, the "likeness of God." In today's passage, a repentant Peter, on fire with the Spirit, fearlessly proclaimed that Jesus the Nazarene was risen. Jesus lives, and so too do we. That is the Easter message (Acts 2:14, 22–33).

The letter of Peter explores the perishable and imperishable things of life. Peter contended that perishable stuff like silver or gold doesn't free us from death or nothingness. No! The imperishable blood of Jesus, the lamb of God, freed us from death so we can be in a relationship with God forever (1 Pt 1:17–21).

And so, with the eyes of faith fixed on this imperishable prize, Jesus challenges us to live a life worthy of our baptismal calling. Never give up on our calling. Persevere!

The author of the Lukan gospel describes two disciples on their way to Emmaus who initially didn't recognize Jesus, even as they were walking and talking with him. These disciples presumably knew Jesus and probably believed he was a "prophet mighty in deed and word." But now they were disheartened, perhaps even disillusioned, as they walked. And they probably were confused; they had heard rumors that Jesus was alive. Was he, or wasn't he? Eventually in the "breaking of the bread" (a phrase for the Eucharist) they recognize with their eyes of faith the transfigured reality of Jesus Christ. They were seeking God and found him in the "breaking of the bread" (Lk 24:13–35).

I like to think that God reveals himself to us if we persistently seek him.

Yes, we seek God in prayer, especially in the Mass. But we should also seek God's wisdom in the Bible, his Spirit in trying to do the right thing, and his presence in our daily routine.

Yes, seek God's wisdom in the prayerful reading of the Bible, a privileged expression of our faith. God is the author in that it highlights what God wants us to know about himself, his relationship with the universe, and his purpose for us. The Bible is about religious, not scientific, truths. The many biblical authors communicated these religious truths through the languages, images, and literary forms with which they were familiar. At the heart of the Bible is the Christian belief that Jesus, the incarnate Word of God, entered our history so we could become like God. Jesus Christ is our way into the future, our truth who exemplifies our true self, and our life in and through and with whom we breathe and live. Yes, we open the Bible to hear from God about the baffling questions of life: Who am I really? What is the purpose of my life? How should I live? Why is there evil?

Seeking God requires discipline and patience. That's why we pray for the grace to seek God daily, to wait patiently and listen to him.

Second, seek God's Spirit persistently. Jesus encourages us to pray. He explained the importance of persistence in our relationship with God. Keep on asking … keep on seeking … keep on knocking … "For everyone who asks, receives; and the one who seeks, finds; and to the one who knocks, the door will be opened." Isn't that what Luke 11:9 and onward are all about?

Yes, we may have doubts about this. We may even wonder, *If I ask, will I receive?* We may find it difficult to believe that God would give us anything, let alone something as wonderful as his Spirit and the gifts of his Spirit. For example, wisdom to know what truly matters, knowledge, and understanding to delve into the mysteries of God and the truths of our faith, courage to stand up for what's right, and so forth. Remember, Jesus emphasized, "How much more will the Father in heaven give the Holy Spirit to *those who ask him?*" (Lk 11:13, emphasis mine). Obviously, we should seek the right things. But the point is this: never give up seeking God, his kingdom, his grace, and his Spirit.

Finally, seek God's presence enthusiastically in our daily routine.

We live in a world that thinks the only thing that matters is how we relate to other people. How we relate to others is tremendously important and is the subject of seven out of the ten commandments. However, our relationship with God is the most important aspect of life. It is out of this relationship that our love for others should flow—our relationships in our family and then our relationships with others.

Like the search for the Egyptian tombs, we must be persistent in the pursuit of our ultimate purpose in life. Seek God daily, persistently, and enthusiastically as the disciples did; and we will find God in all his fullness, and his life—divine life—will transform us into new creatures in the way we love and serve one another. And even if we fall or stumble, if we seek God, he will lift us up, as God lifted Peter up, so we can discover and enjoy our true treasure: God and the things of God.

FOURTH SUNDAY OF EASTER

I read about a Florida senior citizen who bought a new Corvette, drove it onto I-95, and soon was speeding at eighty miles per hour. In his rearview mirror, he saw a state trooper, lights flashing and siren blaring. The man floored the pedal to ninety miles per hour. Suddenly he thought, *What am I doing? I'm too old for this juvenile behavior!* He pulled over.

The trooper walked up and said, "Sir, my shift ends in thirty minutes. If you can give me a new reason for speeding that I've never heard before, I'll let you go."

The man paused and then said, "My wife ran off with a state trooper, and I thought you were trying to bring her back to me."

"Have a good day, sir," replied the trooper. Now that's creative thinking!

The word of God takes us back to the beginnings of Christianity, to the outpouring of the Spirit on the disciples, to Peter courageously and boldly proclaiming that Jesus is risen and alive, the Messiah, the fulfillment of the hopes of ancient Israel (Acts 2:14, 36–41).

Peter concluded that we should reform our lives, be baptized, and live an others-centered, God-centered life. Peter's question to us may be, What kind of life are we living?

The letter of Peter encourages a persecuted community to see Jesus as their model. Suffering is ultimately a mystery. It's also inescapable, like the other two inescapables of life—guilt and death. The author here proclaimed that the mystery of suffering, accepted in faith, can bring about healing for others. Why so? Because that's what the suffering of Jesus did. It restored our relationship with God: God in us and we in God. (1 Pt 2:20–25).

The gospel portrays Jesus as the good shepherd, the gate into eternal life. It gives us many images of Jesus. He is the bread; the vine; the way, the truth, and the life; the gate; the door; the resurrection; and the good shepherd. These so-called seven "I am" sayings allude to the divinity of Jesus (Jn 10:1–10).

I particularly like the image of Jesus as the "door" to eternal life. We pass through many doors in our lives, don't we? The open door welcomes friends, fresh air, and warm light. Yes, we're open—come on in! The open door is the sure sign that we belong, that we have a place. And the closed door shelters and protects us.

Architects sometimes spend a great deal of time and money designing the entry or facade of construction projects. They want to make a statement. Doors can speak for us as well. They can be opened in an act of compassion. They can be slammed in anger. In the corporate world, a door may indicate status; power rests with the one who has the key. The doors we pass through may be transitions from fear into safety, from isolation into community, and from struggle into peace. The church door welcomes us into God's presence. The courthouse door may be the entry into righting wrongs, seeking justice, or protecting the common good. The college or university door is the threshold into learning and discovery. Our own front door is the assurance that we are safely home.

In today's gospel, Jesus called himself the "gate," the entry way to God, the "door" through which we pass from this transitory, fragile, earthly life into a transfigured heavenly one. It's an evolutionary leap from one kind of existence into another. On our journey to the fullness of the kingdom of God, Jesus is our gateway into truth, justice, peace, and life in all its fullness. What a magnificent image of Jesus: the door into eternal life.

The Easter season is all about life and hope. In Jesus's death on Good Friday is hidden his glorious resurrection at Easter. Yes, Jesus Christ lives, and because he lives, we live. The Easter season challenges us to reset our lives each day. Every day is a new beginning.

But how make of a fresh start do we have each day? A best seller titled *Make Your Bed: Little Things That Can Change Your Life ... and Maybe the World* offers some advice. The author, William McRaven, led the manhunt that tracked down Osama Bin Laden. He cited ten little things, life lessons, that aren't little at all. Here are some:

—First, make your bed every morning, because when you accomplish one thing early in the day, you'll be motivated to achieve more. The point is, if you don't do the little things right, you won't do the big things right. Start each day with a task completed.

—To change the world, find someone to help you paddle, a friend or colleague who can mentor you from goals to achievement because you can't accomplish much on your own.

—Always measure a person by the size of his or her heart, not by physical size, skin color, creed, or anything else. Respect everyone. But what matters most is the will to succeed.

—Remember, life isn't fair, but that's no reason to cry. Keep going. Keep moving forward despite failures, because every life has failures, and what you learn from failures will make you wiser. Take risks, because life is a struggle; and without challenges, you'll never realize your potential.

—Stand up to the bullies. There are a lot of sharks in the world, and we have to deal with them.

In your darkest moments, you must be your very best—calm, composed, and strategic—so you can bring all your skills of mind and strength of character to bear on the challenge before you. And make others believe in a brighter day. Never underestimate the power of hope.

Yes, *Make Your Bed* has several life lessons about how to begin every day.

One person can change the world by giving people hope. Think, for example, of Abraham Lincoln, Mahatma Gandhi, Franklin Roosevelt, Winston Churchill, Martin Luther King, Nelson Mandela, Mother Teresa, and of course, Jesus Christ. Not all our dreams will come true, but some will if we persevere.

The Easter season is about hope; it's about hope in God. To paraphrase the author of the letter of John, what we shall be has not yet been revealed. We shall be like God, for we shall see God as he really is (1 Jn 3:2).

Yes, at every stage in our earthly pilgrimage through death into eternal life, God is present invisibly. As St. Paul put it, "At present we see indistinctly, as in a mirror, but then face to face" (1 Cor. 13:12).

Seeing God face-to-face is the fulfillment of our hope. In the meantime, let us pursue every opportunity, to paraphrase John Wesley, to do all the good we can. By all means we can. In all the ways we can. In all the places we can. At all the times we can. To all the people we can. As long as ever we can.

May our hope in God always guide us to look for the good in people instead of harping on the worst; to discover what can be done instead of grumbling about what cannot; and to be a good loser because we have the divine assurance of final victory. Yes, Jesus Christ is risen. And because he lives, we live.

Fifth Sunday of Easter

Today we celebrate Mother's Day.

I think everyone would agree that mothers are great teachers. Here are a few things my mother taught me:

She taught me to appreciate a job well done. She would say to us, for example, "If you're going to kill each other, do it outside; I just finished cleaning!"

Mom taught logic. How many have I heard Mom say, "Because I said so, that's why"?

Mom gave lessons about the economy—for example, "Clean your room. We don't have a maid in our budget."

And about envy, she would say, "There are millions of starving children who don't have a supper like yours!" Do these lessons sound familiar?

Seriously the words *mother* and *mom* evoke many roles, but whatever her job, a mother shows her children how to live. And what's the most important thing a mother can give? Unconditional love, acceptance, and forgiveness. Our mothers encourage us, are patient, and are always ready to listen. Yes, we never will be able to fully measure the unconditional love of a mother for her child.

The word of God in the book of Acts takes us back to the beginnings of Christianity. The early church was beginning to diversify—Gentiles as well as Jews, Greek-speaking as well as Aramaic-speaking disciples. The challenge then and now is how to stay united as the church diversifies. Suddenly in this passage, a problem arises. The community is neglecting the needy. But they don't let the problem simmer. They solve it. They ordain some as deacons. The Greek word *diakonia* means "service" (Acts 6:1–7).

It wouldn't surprise me if Stephen Covey was inspired by this passage to publish his best seller *The Seven Habits of Highly Effective People*. He added an eighth. This best seller is worth rereading. These habits help whenever we face problems.

Remember the saying "I shall pass through this world but once. Any good therefore that I can do or any kindness that I can show to any human being, let me do it now. Let me not defer or neglect it, for I shall not pass this way again."

The letter of Peter evokes the image of a building, a spiritual house, a cathedral, a living temple of God. The living Christ is the cornerstone or center; and we, the community of believers, are the living stones of that house. Churches evoke for me images of the great medieval Gothic cathedrals, with stain-glassed windows that tell the biblical story of salvation, vaulted ceilings that lift our eyes upward to God, stone-carved biblical heroes and heroines who inspire, and brilliant light that symbolizes Jesus Christ (1 Pt 2:4–9).

The author of Peter challenges us to build a living temple to God, a cathedral, so to speak, out of our lives of discipleship with Jesus. The stones are our good deeds, for as folk wisdom goes, in death, the only things we take with us are our good deeds.

In the gospel, Jesus said we have a dwelling place with God. What precisely will this dwelling place be like? We don't know. Death is our most radical act of faith in God. It's like a trapeze. We let go of our earth-bound existence, all we call human life, our very selves with unconditional trust. God will catch us in that great leap into darkness and bear us away within himself forever (Jn 14:1–12).

Today I would like to look at images of the church in light of Peter's letter. One of my favorites, one of the oldest, is a boat, which offers so many insights into who the church is and the history of the church. Imagine! We're in a boat. We're on a journey together with a map and lots of stormy weather, with people slipping overboard, survivors being pulled in, mutinies occurring among the crew, the ship getting off course, and fears of being attacked. And a boat needs a captain when everybody's losing his or her heads. He may not be ideal—too lax, too strict—but if everybody grabs the tiller, we're all in trouble. Peter, for example, didn't seem to be the ideal captain, yet what his crew and subsequent crews managed to do has lasted over two thousand years and today has 1.3 billion people, plus three hundred million orthodox and eight hundred million Protestants under the umbrella of "Christianity."

There are many models of this church—an institution with a structure, the mystical body or people of God, a servant, the herald of the good news, and the sacrament or sign of God's grace. No one model can fully capture the reality of the church.

Perhaps we might best describe the church as a community of those who believe in God as triune and in Jesus Christ as the Son of God and the redeemer of humankind. They shape their lives according to that belief; they are a community that remembers that belief ritually in the Eucharist and recognizes the Bishop of Rome as the foundation of its unity.

This global community of believers lives under a huge tent. Some people are good; others are not so good. In fact, some are downright dysfunctional. They make a mess out of their lives and the lives of others. They sometimes even leave a mess. And so, like so many other things in life, the church lives with some messiness and muddles through as best it can. But we continually must strive to do the right thing, to forgive ourselves and one another, to let go of feelings of resentment and bitterness, and to get our lives back on track. And as the prophet Micah said centuries before Jesus, we should "do the right and love goodness and walk humbly with our God."

And what does this community of believers do? We remember and celebrate the awesome presence of the living Christ in our midst. He is our way into eternal life, our truth who scatters the "fake news" all around us, and our life who overcomes death. We retell the stories of Jesus; we celebrate the sacramental presence of the living Christ in liturgical signs, such as baptismal water, Eucharistic bread and wine, and healing consecratory oil. The same Spirit who transformed the disciples from cowards hiding behind closed doors into heroes, proclaiming fearlessly that Jesus is alive, is the same Spirit who lives within our global community, within us. He can fire us up to do wonders for God if we will only let the Spirit do so.

In the final analysis, we are a global community of believers that stretches back to the first century of our Christian era. We will continue into this millennium and perhaps into many more until Jesus Christ triumphantly returns in his Second Coming to transform this universe into a "new heaven and a new earth."

In the meantime, to paraphrase Teresa of Avila, the living Christ has no body but ours—no hands, no feet, but ours. Ours are the eyes with which the living Christ looks compassionately on the needy. Ours are the feet with which he walks to do good, and ours are the hands with which he helps others.

Sixth Sunday of Easter

I heard about a husband and wife (I'll simply refer to them as Joe and Mary) who flew from Florida to Australia for a vacation to celebrate their fortieth wedding anniversary. As the plane was crossing the Pacific, the captain suddenly announced, "Ladies and gentlemen, I am afraid I have some very bad news. Our engines are malfunctioning, and so we're going to attempt an emergency landing. Luckily, I see an uncharted island, and we should be able to land on the beach. But the odds are that we may never be found!"

The plane landed safely on the island. Joe, shaken, turned to his wife and asked, "Mary, did we pay our pledge to the 'Forward in Faith' appeal yet?" She responded, "No, sweetheart." Joe asked, "Did we pay the annual pastoral appeal?" She said, "I'm sorry. I forgot to send the check." "And, Mary, did you remember to send a check to our pastor for the building fund?" "Forgive me, Joe," Mary pleaded. "I didn't." Joe gave her the biggest kiss in forty years. Mary, startled, asked, "Why?" Joe answered, "We're not stuck on this island. The bishop and pastor will find us to get those payments." Guess what: they found them.

According to a United Nations statistic, there were approximately fourteen million refugees around the world in 2016. These are men, women, and children forced to flee their homelands under the threat of persecution, conflict, or violence. Perhaps the most shocking photo was of a three-year-old Syrian boy washed up on a beach, lying face down in the surf, not far from a fashionable resort in Turkey. Another iconic image showed the inconsolable father of this boy. The father looked so helpless and alone.

Today Jesus called forth a similar, but not so shocking, image of loss when he announced his departure from the disciples, his close friends. Jesus was about to leave them, and they felt helpless and alone. But Jesus promised that he would still be with them through the Spirit.

So what else does the word of God say to us today?

The word carries us back in our imaginations to the beginnings of Christianity, to a deacon named Philip, who was traveling to the back-water city of Samaria. And what was Philip doing? Despite a local persecution, Philip was proclaiming the good news that Jesus Christ lives. And because he lives, we live. Philip had such remarkable success as an exorcist, healer, and baptizer that the Jerusalem community dispatched Peter and John to Samaria so they could "lay hands on them"—in other words, breathe the Spirit on these newly baptized and fire them up with the gifts of the Spirit. These gifts were wisdom (to recognize what truly matters in life), intelligence (to discern what's true), courage (to stand up for what's right), empathy or compassion (to see the needy), good judgment (to do right), and wonder and awe (to worship the great God of this universe) (Acts 8:5–8, 14–17).

The author may be asking us whether we're fired up with the gifts of the Spirit and reflect them in our attitudes and behaviors.

The letter of Peter urges Christians to be patient, especially in adversity, and to speak with "gentleness and reverence." Like Jesus, if they must suffer, he asks them to suffer for doing good rather than for doing evil. Because the innocent Jesus also suffered for the guilty. God exalted him through the life-giving Spirit, and God also will exalt us (1 Pt 3:15–18).

In the Gospel according to John, the author alluded to the mystery of the triune God: Father, Son, and Spirit. The triune God lives within us, and we live within the triune God. This is called the "mystery of the indwelling of God." His presence is as real to us now as it was to the disciples then. But the challenge is to find the presence of God in our daily lives (Jn 14:15–21).

I would like to highlight how a book titled *Grace's Window* discerns the mysterious presence of God in everyday life at a hospital.

The author notes that the hospital confounds the peaceful soul with the realization that the God of daily living is also the God of sudden dying. The God of the comfortable parish sanctuary is also the God of intensive care. The God of candle and incense is the God of diseases; the God of music is the God of squeaky gurney wheels and crying children. The God of wine and bread is the God of wounded flesh and blood.

The God of all these smells, sights, and sounds is also the God of profound silence. When despair prevents ordinary prayer, when the psalms fail and words seem meaningless, the mantle of loneliness becomes "a mantle of dark and wordless love," as Suzanne Guthrie wrote.

This very simple yet profound point is also the point of today's gospel. We tend to isolate God to "church" or "temple," to remove God from our work week. But God is in all of life: in moments of great joy, in periods of dark sadness, in the nitty-gritty of daily work, and in times of doubt and disappointment. The gospel especially invites us to look beneath and beyond the ordinary appearances of daily life that envelop us and see the reality of God all around us. And so, as you plan ways to spend your day, I share some tips from the Zambian poet Martin Greyford.

> Take time to think.
> It is the source of all power.
> Take time to read.
> It is the foundation of wisdom.
> Take time to pray.
> It is the greatest power on earth.
> Take time to give.
> It is too short a day to be selfish.

I conclude with inspiration from Theodore Roosevelt, a "renaissance man" and a naturalist, Phi Beta Kappa Harvard graduate, rancher, author, conservationist, historian, politician, "Rough Riders" colonel, Nobel Peace Prize winner, intellectual, explorer, public official, statesman, and the twenty-sixth president of the United States. At forty-two, he was the youngest president ever.

Roosevelt stated, "A thorough knowledge of the Bible is worth more than a college education." He based his philosophy of life on what he called "realizable ideals," and he believed that we find ourselves by being involved with institutions, people, jobs, causes, movements, and everyday life. Roosevelt was, as he said, the person "in the arena whose face is marred by dust and sweat and blood; who strives valiantly; who knows the great enthusiasms; who spends himself on a worthy cause; who at best knows the triumph of high achievement, and who at the worst, if he fails, at least fails while daring greatly so that his place will never be with those cold and timid souls who know neither victory or defeat."

Yes, let us find the presence of God everywhere, especially in the nitty-gritty of daily work.

ASCENSION OF THE LORD
(SEVENTH SUNDAY OF EASTER)

F riday was the last day of school for our St. Raphael students. Youngsters often say things as they plainly see them. For example, a little girl, attending a wedding for the first time, whispered to her mother, "Why is the bride dressed in white?" The mother replied, "Because white is the color of happiness, and today is the happiest day of her life." The little girl thought for a moment and then asked, "So why is the groom in black?"

It's also a holiday weekend—a time to enjoy the outdoors. You may have heard about two college students who went hiking and suddenly encountered a bear. One quickly put his running shoes on. The other said, "You don't think you'll outrun the bear?" The other replied, "I don't have to outrun the bear; I only have to outrun you!" Quick thinking!

This Monday the nation honors the men and women who died in the wars of our country. Some may remember the adage "If the country is good enough to live in, it's good enough to fight for." Washington, DC, a city of monuments, will be at the center of many tributes. When I went to DC and had time, I occasionally stopped by the Vietnam Memorial.

On the 492-foot long, V-shaped black granite wall are fifty-eight-thousand-plus names. Occasionally I read a letter at the foot of the wall a soldier had written home. And I thought, *How many hopes lie buried here?* And then I thought about the Easter season. Our faith assures us that Jesus Christ through his death and resurrection reconnected us to

God, that God's life bestowed on us in baptism and nourished in the sacraments won't disappear. No, in the mystery of death, we will make an evolutionary leap into a new kind of spiritual embodiment. What that is we really don't know.

During these last forty some days, we have been celebrating different aspects of the one paschal or Passover mystery—not only the death and resurrection of Jesus but also his ascension or return to his Father in glory and the descent of the Spirit of God on the disciples at Pentecost. This passage of Jesus from an earthy life into a new, transfigured heavenly reality anticipates our own transformation. The ascension is Jesus's final leave-taking from his community of disciples so that something new can happen: the descent of the Spirit. Yes, the living Christ continues among us and is incredibly active but henceforth through the power, energy, vitality, and force of the Spirit.

Now what does the word of God have to say to us?

The author of the book of Acts flat out indicates that the Lukan gospel and the Acts of the Apostles are a two-volume work. The gospel is about Jesus; Acts is about early Christianity (Acts 1:1–11).

The ascension connects Luke and Acts. It signals the close of Jesus's earthly ministry and heralds the beginning of the church's ministry by the power of the Spirit—the proclamation of the good news that Jesus Christ is alive. He lives; and because he lives, we live.

In his letter to the Christian community at Ephesus, Paul prayed that we will grow in true wisdom and spiritual enlightenment so we will more clearly see God's saving work in Jesus Christ. Jesus is indeed the "head" of the "body," the church, the people of God, you and me. And with our multi talents, we are called to build up this mystical body of Christ (Eph 1:17–23).

In the Gospel according to Matthew, Jesus told the disciples to be missionary disciples. The disciples, you and I, are now the hands and feet and eyes and ears and voice of the living Christ until he comes again in glory to transform this universe into a "new heaven and a new earth" (Mt 28:16–20).

So, what is this church, this worldwide community of disciples to which we belong? A while ago, thirty-five of us parishioners made a stirring pilgrimage to central Italy. We saw Assisi, Florence, Siena, and Rome—to name some sites. In Rome, we participated in a papal audience in St. Peter's Square with thousands from all over the world. We even saw the motorcade of the U.S. president.

Luckily, we stood about ten feet from Pope Francis in his pope mobile. He is indeed a friendly, compassionate face for the church universal. Afterward, I reflected on this global Catholic community and what I like about it.

First, we are a community of disciples who remember and celebrate the awesome presence of Jesus Christ—our way into eternity with God, our truth that scatters falsehood, and our life that overcomes death. We retell the stories of Jesus, and we celebrate the presence of the living Christ all around us, especially in people, in the Bible, and in liturgical signs, such as water, bread and wine, and oil. The living Christ through the power of the Spirit lives within this community, within you and me, and the power, energy, force, and vitality of the Spirit can fire us up to do wonders for God.

The second thing I like about belonging to this worldwide community of disciples is that we are a family. We are sons and daughters of God our Father. Oh yes, we argue about this or that, but don't all families? An argument can be a good sign that we care enough to disagree about something. We are a global family that stretches back to early Christianity. It's a family that will continue into this millennium and perhaps many more. This family lives under a huge tent or umbrella. Yes, some are good, and others are not so good; in fact, some are downright dysfunctional. Yet we must strive to do the right thing, despite falls or lapses. We must continually forgive ourselves and one another, let go of burdens of guilt for behaviors done or not done, let go of bitterness for wrongs done to us, and get our lives back on track. Every day should be a fresh start into eternity.

A third thing I like about belonging to this Catholic family is that we take a stand on peace and justice. I think of the statements of Pope Francis. I think of shelters, hospices, soup kitchens, literacy programs, immigration services, day care centers, hospitals, and schools all over the world that our Catholic community sponsors. I also think of international agencies, such as Catholic Relief Services, Caritas, and the Catholic Agency for Overseas Development, to name a few.

My friends, we should be proud to belong to this worldwide community of disciples. It is indeed a community that remembers and celebrates the presence of the living Christ. It is a family that strives to do the right thing, despite falls and lapses.

May the living Christ inspire us to become coworkers with God in doing all the good we can. By all the means we can. In all the ways we can. In all the places we can. At all the times we can. To all the people we can. As long as ever we can.

PENTECOST SUNDAY

One Sunday, as people filed out of a church, a pastor noticed a youngster staring at a large plaque. It was etched with the names of men and women who had died in the wars of our nation. The pastor greeted the youngster, who asked, "Why are these names here?" The pastor replied, "It is a memorial to the men and women who died in the service." The youngster paused and then asked, "Which church service was that?" Let's hope that doesn't happen today.

Today we celebrate Pentecost, the outpouring of the Spirit on the disciples gathered in Jerusalem centuries ago. The lesson of Pentecost is simple yet profound: the triune God lives in us and we in God. To paraphrase St. Paul, we are living temples of God.

Pentecost isn't easy to celebrate visually. In Advent, for example, we see a wreath. At Christmas we see the crib and the tree. In Lent we focus on the cross and the cactus as a reminder of our forty-day desert journey. At Easter, we have a paschal candle and display lilies. But except for red vestments, which symbolize tongues of fire, there's not much to see on Pentecost Sunday.

It wasn't always so. In some medieval churches, people dropped burning straw from the ceiling to recreate the "fiery tongues" at Pentecost. That practice stopped when it set some churches afire. And there was the dove, which symbolized the Spirit in light of Luke's description of Jesus's baptism in the Jordan. In medieval France, white pigeons were released in cathedrals during the singing of the hymn "Come, Holy Spirit." But that was discontinued when people complained that something other than the Holy Spirit was dropping from the rafters.

The image I like best is "breath of God" or "gush of wind." It's something you feel. It's catching the Spirit. It's feeling the Spirit of God moving wherever it wants to recreate whatever it touches. Remember, for example, how the "dry bones" in the book of Ezekiel felt God's Spirit bringing them back to life. The power, force, energy, and vitality of the Spirit are within us. It moves us or "seizes us" so we can be a channel of love, joy, peace, patience, kindness, generosity, gentleness, faithfulness, and self-discipline to one another.

Pentecost concludes the Easter season and begins the mission of the church, the people of God, you and me, to continue the saving work of Jesus Christ until he comes again in great glory and power at the end-time. And one way we can continue that saving work is by embodying the following gifts of the Spirit: wisdom (recognizing what truly matters in life), intelligence (discerning what's true), courage (standing up for what's right), empathy or compassion (caring for the needy), good judgment (doing the right thing), and wonder and awe (worshipping the great God of this universe).

The word *Pentecost* comes from a Greek word meaning "fiftieth" for the fiftieth day after the Hebrew Passover. The Hebrews initially celebrated this festival after harvesting the spring wheat in their fields. Later the Hebrews associated this festival with the covenant God had made with their forebears on Mt. Sinai—a covenant summed up very simply yet very powerfully in the phrase "You are my people and I am your God."

In the Christian tradition, Pentecost gradually celebrated one aspect of the entire paschal mystery, including the death, resurrection, ascension of Jesus, and descent of the Spirit.

The book of Acts describes how the Jews had come to Jerusalem to celebrate the festival of Pentecost. And suddenly the Spirit—described in images of wind and fire (images that symbolize power, force, energy, and vitality)—was poured out on the disciples and emboldened them to preach the gospel fearlessly in Jerusalem and eventually to people all over the Mediterranean (Acts 2:1–11).

The word of God asks us, "Do we stand up for what's right?" I always remember that great philosophical clarion call "If not you, who? And if not now, when?"

The letter of Paul to the Christian community at Corinth in Greece speaks about all the gifts the Spirit bestows on us, all for the common good. In our own twenty-first century, when we often overemphasize the individual, Paul's words are a powerful reminder to seek the common good (1 Cor 12:3–7, 12–13).

Some of you may have heard of *The Paradoxical Commandments.* In this age of the World Wide Web, someone picked up this paper and circulated it, and it began circling the globe, attributed to everyone from Mother Teresa to psychiatrist Karl Menninger. The greatest paradox was discovering it had been written in 1968 by a college student no one had ever heard of. Here are some of *The Paradoxical Commandments.* I like to think St. Paul would have agreed with them considering today's passage.

> People are illogical, unreasonable, and self-centered;
> Love them anyway.
>
> If you do good, people will accuse you of selfish, ulterior motives; Do good anyway.
>
> The biggest men and women with the biggest ideas can be shot down by the smallest men and women with the smallest minds; Think big anyway.
>
> People favor underdogs, but follow only top dogs; Fight for the underdogs anyway.
>
> What you spend years building may be destroyed in one night; Build anyway.
>
> People really need help but may attack you if you do help them; Help people anyway.

Doing these paradoxical acts will serve the common good Paul highlighted in his letter.

The Gospel according to John describes a post-resurrection

appearance of Jesus, when he breathed on the disciples (as God breathed life into us in the book of Genesis), and in that gesture he bestowed the Spirit on the disciples (Jn 20:19–23).

So you may ask, "What does the Spirit of God do within us?"

It's a tremendous truth: the God of the universe, the triune God, lives within us. Because he is there, we are new creatures. We have a destiny, eternal life with God. That life has already begun. And if you want to see what the Spirit can do, look at the early disciples; they were transformed from cowards into heroes.

Let us pray on this feast that the Spirit, whose gifts we already possess, will empower us to live the results of the Spirit's presence in us. Those are love, joy, peace, patience, kindness, generosity, gentleness, faithfulness, and self-discipline, which St. Paul described so powerfully.

The same Spirit of God who spoke through the prophets of ancient Israel, who overshadowed the Virgin Mary, who descended on the disciples, and who lives within the church—the community of believers—guides human history despite its twists and turns toward its ultimate fulfillment.

That Spirit lives within you and me and can transform us if we will let him.

THE MOST HOLY TRINITY

I recently read about a woman who was a fantastic organizer. She even prepaid her own funeral expenses. But she didn't like the headstone at her husband's grave, so she handed her daughter $3,000 to buy "a lovely stone." A year after she died, one of her sons stopped at the grave site before he went to his sister's home for dinner. He saw the same old stone at the grave. He asked his sister, "Didn't Mom ask you to buy a new stone?" The sister replied, "Yes. I'm wearing it on my finger … *a lovely stone.*" So much for miscommunication!

Today we celebrate the mystery of the triune God, a fundamental truth of Christianity. One God in three is completely beyond us and yet completely within us. To put this mystery simply, the God of this universe, a God of wonder and awe, became flesh in Jesus (the mystery of the incarnation, a second fundamental truth) and lives among us by the power of the Spirit. Yes, that's one God in three distinct modes or movements—Father, Son, and Spirit. And that's why we begin prayer in the name of the Father, Son, and Holy Spirit.

One of my favorite Broadway musicals is *Godspell*, especially the song adapted from a prayer attributed to the thirteenth-century Saint Richard of Chichester. "O dear Lord three things I pray: to see thee more clearly, love thee more dearly, and follow thee more nearly, day by day." This is a powerful prayer in an age when many people don't believe in God or live as though there's no God. I, of course, think Blaise Pascal, a seventeenth-century mathematician and philosopher, got it right. "Pascal's Wager" says,

One does not know whether God exists;
not believing in God is bad for one's eternal soul if God
does exist;
believing in God is of no consequence if God does not
exist;
therefore it is in one's interest to believe in God.

Think about it!

In our better moments, or when some crisis may begin to overwhelm us, we may think about fundamental questions such as, What is the meaning of life? What is my purpose? Surely, we can't be content with the adage "Eat, drink and be merry," or worse, the seventeenth-century philosopher Thomas Hobbes's judgment that life is "nasty, brutish and short." No. Bad stuff like suffering and evil cry out for Someone greater than ourselves. The will to live requires that we discover some purpose for living. I would argue, as Pascal did, that within each of us is a space that "can be filled only with an infinite and immutable object; in other words by God himself" (*Pensées VII*).

Pascal likely read St. Augustine, who wrote in his autobiographical *Confessions*, "You have formed us for Yourself, and our hearts are restless till they find rest in You." Yes, we were born to live in relationship with God—the triune God—and that's what today's feast highlights.

The word of God takes us back over three thousand years to a key moment in salvation history, the Exodus or the liberation of the Hebrews from Egypt. God called Moses to Mount Sinai a second time (after the Hebrews had broken their covenant) and revealed he was a merciful, compassionate, and faithful God. Moses then begged God to dwell with his people. And God did (Ex 34:4–6, 8–9). We might ask, How faithful are we to our baptismal promises? Do we live as sons or daughters of God?

In his farewell letter, Paul appealed to the Christian community in Corinth to live a godlike life and then blessed them with that introductory prayer we hear so often at the beginning of this liturgy (2 Cor 13:11–13). Paul might ask us, Do we try to live godlike lives? Do we practice the virtues in our daily lives?

In the Gospel according to John, the author described God as the "Tremendous Lover" who became one of us so we might have eternal life

(Jn 3:16–18). The question for us is, Do we live our lives in light of our ultimate purpose: eternal life with God and one another?

The mystery of the triune God—a God utterly beyond us and yet utterly within us, a God who is one as well as diverse, a God of distinctive relationships—invites us to ask ourselves, What kind of a relationship do we have with God?

Most people have a relationship with God that is perhaps more subconscious than conscious. And why do I say this? Because we are forever trying to find answers to those fundamental questions of human life that people often ask in moments of crisis—for example, the death of a family member, a life-threatening illness, a broken marriage, the loss of a job or savings, misunderstandings, and so forth. In moments such as these, people often ask questions such as, What is the purpose of my life? Where is my life going? Does anyone care what happens to me? These are religious questions, questions we cannot help but try to answer.

As we grow old, we may wonder, What was my life all about? We appear to have accomplished so little, and now it is almost over.

Moreover, life seems to be filled with so many tragedies—senseless murders in our streets, mindless violence in failed states, and natural disasters everywhere.

But we also have those occasional experiences that shake us out of our dull routine—moments of awe and wonder, and not necessarily a spectacular experience such as the Grand Canyon or Niagara Falls. Perhaps it's a glorious sunset, the joy of a friendship, or the accomplishment of a goal. Such experiences can lift us out of ourselves into the presence of a power beyond us. We begin to experience the transcendent dimension of our own lives.

Yes, we say, there must be an awesome power beyond us, a purposeful, gracious, and compassionate God who is responsible not only for this incredible universe but also for our own very lives.

Catholic Christianity says our God is indeed a merciful God who can heal the brokenness of human life. This God became flesh in Jesus and is alive among us by the power of the Spirit. That is the mystery of the triune God: Father, Son, and Spirit.

This is the same God who freed the Hebrews from their oppressors in ancient Egypt and who renewed his covenant with them at Sinai.

This God showed his face to us in Jesus of Nazareth. Through him, with him, and in him, we live in God's triune life, and the triune God lives in us.

This triune God, the model of self-giving love, empowers us to reach out in love to one another with compassion, forgiveness, a smile, a kind word, and a helping hand. And in reaching out to one another in love, we become like the triune God in self-giving love.

And so, I come back to *Godspell*. Let us pray on this feast that we might see our triune God more clearly, love God more dearly, and follow God more nearly.

Amen.

THE MOST HOLY BODY AND
BLOOD OF CHRIST

Happy Father's Day! The word *father* or *dad* evokes many memories. When I think of my own father, I think of certain qualities he possessed, qualities all good fathers possess: love (he tried to do what was best for us), commitment (he stuck by us), support (he gave us as much as he could), forgiveness (he wasn't afraid to say he was sorry), communication (he listened to us, especially around the dinner table), spirituality (we went to church together as often as we could), and time (we spent time together). Let's thank God for our dads. I invite all fathers to stand for our applause.

How many remember Yogi Berra? The legendary Yankees catcher is in the Baseball Hall of Fame. I recently saw an article, in which he said, "I really didn't say everything I said." That's one example of his quick wit. For example, "It ain't over 'til it's over; Ninety percent of the game is half mental; You better cut the pizza in four pieces because I'm not hungry enough to eat six." When asked about a popular restaurant, he said, "Nobody goes there anymore, it's too crowded." Finally, there's this quintessential Yogi-ism: "Always go to other people's funerals, otherwise, they won't go to yours." Enjoyable summer reading are Yogi Berra's books.

Today we celebrate the Feast of the Body and Blood of Jesus Christ, the Eucharist, a Greek word meaning "thanksgiving," thanksgiving to God for the gift of salvation, for the gift of living in relationship with God forever.

First, here's a statistic. Of 7.3 billion people living on this planet, over eight hundred million go to bed hungry every night. In other words, imagine seven people at a table. Three load their plates, two get enough, one goes to bed undernourished, and the seventh goes to bed on an empty stomach. But not only do people hunger simply for bread; many hunger for peace, human rights, truth, and God. Check the news for the evidence.

So, what is the role of the Eucharist? The meal table for many is the center of family life. In our global Catholic family, the altar or table of the Lord is the center of our faith community. Think about it.

In some cultures of antiquity, there was a sense of the sacred around the family meal. Life was sacred, and that which nourished life was, therefore, holy as well. At meals they would remember how God had entered their lives and blessed them. Within the simple ritualistic act of eating and drinking, these families celebrated the mysteries of life— marriage, the birth of a child, and the death of a loved one. They would proclaim a belief in immortality by gathering around the table and setting a place for the deceased.

There are numerous opportunities in our own lives for such special and sacred meals: birthdays, anniversaries, marriages, graduations, and great holiday feasts, such as Christmas, Thanksgiving, and Easter. The occasions are as numerous as our imaginations will allow.

The family table is the place where people often gather in love, friendship, and conversation; it stands at the center of home. So too the altar or table of the Lord stands at the center of church.

What does the word of God say to us on this Feast of Corpus Christi, the body and blood of Christ?

The word takes us back to the wanderings of the Hebrews in the wilderness after their escape or exodus from their oppressors. Moses experienced the glory or presence of God at Mt. Sinai and renewed the covenant God had made with the Hebrews. Here the author of Deuteronomy noted the hunger of these Hebrews—not only for food but for God. And God provided. As we think of their hunger, may we think of the hunger of so many people today.

Moses here proclaimed that we need God's word to satisfy our spiritual hunger as much as we need food to satisfy our physical hunger.

As we reflect on God's care, we might give thanks to God for his care for us (Dt 8:2–3, 14–16).

In his letter to the Christian community at Corinth in Greece, Paul spoke about the presence of the risen Christ not only in the bread we break but also in one another. We are all one human family. The Eucharist symbolizes our oneness with one another. Unfortunately, the reality often is the opposite (1 Cor 10:16–17).

In the gospel, Jesus said he is the bread of life. And whoever eats this bread has eternal life. This "I am" saying is one of the seven "I am" sayings in John that alludes to the divinity of Jesus (Jn 6:51–58).

The word of God today focuses on three historical moments: the thirteenth century before the Christian era, the first decade of our Christian era, and today. Each is an exodus, a going out.

First is the Hebrew exodus in the thirteenth century BC. The escape of the Hebrews was a wonder of wonders. Their passage over the sea of reeds is a prototype of liberation from slavery to freedom, from darkness to light, from subjection to redemption. That is why in the seder service, faithful Jewish families proclaim, "Therefore it is our duty to thank, praise … and adore the God who did all of these miracles." Each seder or Passover meal thereafter becomes a feast of hope for a messiah who will come.

Second is the exodus of the first century. Paul spoke of a tradition handed on, the saving word he'd "received from the Lord." The lamb God ordered the Hebrews to eat prefigures "the lamb who takes away the sins of the world," Jesus Christ. The bread and wine are the real presence of the living Christ, "flesh and blood," given for and to us. Jesus's Last Supper is the beginning of his own exodus or "going out" from this earthly life to his heavenly Father. This passage is marked with blood, thorns, spittle, lashes, and nails in his hands and feet. Hence, to eat and drink is to "proclaim the death of the Lord until he comes again." Each Eucharist "is a feast of hope which deepens our messianic expectation." The Messiah will come again at the end-time.

Third is our exodus today. In another Johannine passage, chapter 13, Jesus washed the feet of his disciples at his Last Supper and indicated they should follow his example of servant leadership.

The purpose of the Eucharist is to form us into a vibrant faith community. Yes, the Eucharist is the real presence of the living Christ sacramentally and mystically. But the Eucharist is an empty gesture unless we go out from the table of the Lord to feed the hungry. We are called to go from church to community, to wash the feet of our brothers and sisters, so to speak. To paraphrase an old hymn, Christ has no hands but our hands to do his work today. We must be present to others, where they are, in ways that respond to their needs. Then we will experience our own exodus. The Messiah will come to us, and we will bring the Messiah to others. And when this happens, we will experience, like the Hebrews centuries before, a wonder anew.

TWELFTH SUNDAY IN ORDINARY TIME

I n my former work, I often had to speak at alumni gatherings. Sometimes I spoke at gatherings in close geographic proximity to one another. To make sure I wouldn't tell the same stories to the same people at two different gatherings, I asked the alumni director whether some at the one gathering would attend the other. He, with tongue in cheek, assured me, "It is highly unlikely that anyone who heard you speak at the one would hear you again at the other." There's a message in that statement.

In his book *Nine Essential Things I've Learned about Life*, Rabbi Harold Kushner recounts a sermon he gave about forgiveness. He suggests that just as we ask God to forgive us our wrongdoings, so we should forgive people who have wronged us. One listener was upset. She told the rabbi that her husband had left her six years ago, and as a result, she had to work two jobs to pay the bills and put food on the table. And had to explain to her children many times why they couldn't have the things all their friends had.

And then the punch line came. "And you want me to forgive him for what he has done to us?" she asked. The rabbi responded, "That's right. I want you to forgive him for your sake, not for his. Why are you giving him the power to define you as a victim? Why are you giving him the power to define you in terms of what you don't have … instead of what you do have, a loving home and two beautiful children? Do you realize what you are doing? For six years, you've been holding a 'hot coal' in your hand, looking for an opportunity to throw it at him. And for six years, he's been living comfortably. If he is no longer in your house, why are you letting him live rent-free in your head? ... You can evict him."

Yes, anger and self-pity are "demons" that displace peace and joy in our lives. But with gratitude to God for the blessings we have, we can "exorcise" or drive out these demons of anger and self-pity that rob us of joy and peace. By asking for God's mercy and forgiveness for ourselves and the people who have wronged us, we can make a fresh start with our own lives. That is what Paul is about today: through Jesus Christ we have a new beginning.

So, what does the word of God say to us today?

The word carries us back to the seventh century before Jesus (the turbulent 600s in Israel), to a lament of the prophet Jeremiah. But lament quickly became hope. Jeremiah complained to God, "I'm trying to do what you want me to do, God, and yet people are slandering me; they want to murder me; trip me up." But Jeremiah didn't let these problems stop him from continuing his prophetic mission. No matter how bad things got, he would always trust in God. God is with him. Yes, God will rescue him from those who want to do him in (Jer 20:10–13).

Jeremiah exemplified courage and perseverance in doing good in the face of all kinds of obstacles. He may be asking us, Do we always trust in God, especially when things are not going our way? When what is happening is the opposite of what we want to happen?

In his letter to the Christian community at Rome, Paul reflected on the human condition; everywhere he saw violence, death, and injustice. We fell from grace, proclaimed the book of Genesis. "But who can save us?" Paul asked Jesus Christ, of course. Jesus righted our relationship with God and one another. He lives. And because Christ lives, we live in relationship with God (Rom 5:12–15). Paul may be asking us, How are we nurturing that relationship with God?

In the Gospel according to Matthew, Jesus said, "Do not be afraid." Yes, do not be afraid, for example, to do the right thing. Because God is with us. We have the energy of God within us (Mt 10:26–33).

How often do we hear that the world is running out of energy—oil, coal, gas, and so on? How do we ensure sufficient energy to sustain life? Now, we are searching for power "from above," trying to harness the sun.

All of us face a similar problem on a spiritual level. We face challenges. But where do we look for the energy to overcome them? Do we look to ourselves, our intelligence, our entrepreneurial spirit? Or do we look "above" to the living Christ, the Sun of Righteousness?

God through Jesus Christ by the power of the Spirit has given us his energy, power, and strength. That same energy, power, and strength raised Jesus from the dead. When Jesus completed the job he had been given, he cried out, "It is finished" (Jn 19:30). With that, he bowed his head and gave up his own spirit. The gospel emphasizes that Jesus really did die. In the blood and water flowing from Jesus's side, we see a symbol of hope for humanity. The blood symbolizes his life poured out for us; the water symbolizes the Spirit, whose "waters" will cleanse, heal, and energize us. The evidence of the empty tomb and the Jerusalem and Galilee appearances convinced the disciples that Jesus was alive. They "saw and believed" that God's energy, power, and strength had raised Jesus from the dead. Jesus was alive. This was unexpected sunshine for them. Winter was over. Spring had come.

We rightly think of power belonging to God. We easily forget that the same energy, power, and strength that raised Jesus Christ from the dead *now lives in us*. It so possessed the Jerusalem disciples that they started a *spiritual revolution* heard around the world. And the age of miracles isn't over. The proof? An electrician in Poland, a prisoner in South Africa, a nun in Calcutta—Lech Walesa, Nelson Mandela, and St. Teresa—freed Poles from Soviet occupation, gave back to South Africans their fundamental human rights, and restored to suffering and dying people in India and elsewhere their dignity as human beings made in the likeness of God.

That energy, power, and strength of God within us can fire us up to do the right thing just as they fired up the disciples. Starting today, at home or at work or in the community, I hope we will realize that the quality of our lives and soul's destiny is being measured by our godlike attitudes and behaviors. These include going the extra mile to help someone in need, living up to our promises, and working for the common good. It includes trusting always in an all-good and compassionate God

Fr. Kevin E. Mackin, OFM

who is ever near us in the "twists and turns" of life and will guide us safely home to our heavenly dwelling place. Yes, we can do all these things and more if we let that energy, power, and strength of God work in us just as it has worked in holy men and women throughout the ages.

Thirteenth Sunday in
Ordinary Time

Happy Fourth of July weekend. We celebrate the signing of the Declaration of Independence on July 4, 1776, in Philadelphia. That document proclaims aloud, "We hold these truths to be self-evident, that all men are created equal, that they are endowed by their Creator with certain unalienable rights, that among these are life, liberty and the pursuit of happiness." A century ago, Woodrow Wilson said this document is a "program of action" for all people. This weekend, we might rededicate ourselves afresh to these principles for people everywhere and not just in the United States.

As we reflect on our own religious liberties, we might pray for the many people around the world who are being discriminated against, killed, or injured for practicing their faith. These include Coptic Christians in Egypt, Chaldean Christians in Iraq, and Christians in Nigeria, to name but a few. Pray that God will find a safe home for their families. If you are able, you might consider a gift to Catholic Relief Services or the Catholic Near East Welfare Association for these refugees.

First, here's a story. A few of you may know that Joe Torre, the legendary Yankees baseball coach, and I grew up in the same Brooklyn neighborhood. In fact, we both played ball in Marine Park. I of course didn't do as well as Joe.

I was a pitcher. One day I knew I was in trouble when the Little League coach approached the mound and said, "I think I better have someone else relieve you." But I argued, "I struck this guy out last time." "Yes, I know," said the coach, "but this is the same inning, and he's at bat again." It was the beginning of the end of my baseball career.

The word of God takes us back in our imaginations to the ninth century before Jesus, to a holy man by the name of Elisha. A wealthy and childless woman welcomed this "holy person" into her home and offered him room and board. Elisha, not to be outdone, promised that God would bless her with a child. Lo and behold, God blessed her with a son (2 Kgs 4:8–11, 14–16). The woman invites us to be always hospitable; Elisha was invited to trust in God's providence or care for us as we journey through life.

Paul in his letter described that we have the life of God in us through the waters of baptism (Rom 6:3–4, 8–11). Water can be life threatening as well as life giving. In early Christianity, baptismal candidates submerged or "buried" themselves in a pool of water, a gesture symbolizing a dying to a self-centered life; and as the candidates came up out of the water, that symbolized rising to an others-centered, God-centered life. Paul challenged us to remember our own baptismal promises and who we are: sons and daughters of God our Father, called to live a godlike life.

In the Gospel according to Matthew, Jesus called us to get our priorities straight. First things first is our relationship with God. Then Jesus invited us to see the face of God in our fellow human beings, no matter how hidden that face of God may be (Mt 10:37–42).

During these days we have been celebrating the lives of some of the giants or heroes of our faith, including John the Baptist, Peter, and Paul.

Peter and Paul were two ordinary people who did extraordinary things, two martyrs who lived and died for the gospel: one by crucifixion, the other by beheading. Peter was the rock, the leader; he was often spontaneous and unthinking but always ready to admit a mistake, to make amends. He was someone you could trust.

And Paul, the preacher, the apostle to the Gentiles, often argumentative and aggressive, was always courageous in speaking the truth.

Who are your heroes and heroines in Catholic Christianity? One of my favorite heroes is John the Baptist.

John is called the "Baptist" because he immersed people in the

Jordan River as a sign of repentance, a sign of their desire to be cleansed from old ways so they could live a new way, oriented to God's covenant. John is the one who prepared the way for Jesus, the bridge between the two covenants that created a special relationship between God and us—that of the Hebrews and that of Jesus Christ. John definitely wasn't into fashion. He lived a rugged, ascetic lifestyle, dressing in camel skin and eating locusts and wild honey. And his message in the wilderness was very simple. He proclaimed what the prophet Micah had begged the Hebrews to do centuries before: do what is right, love goodness, and walk humbly with your God. "Repent," John cried out. "Orient your life to God's covenant."

Most importantly, John pointed to Jesus as the light, the Lord, the One to whom we owe our ultimate allegiance, the "Passover" or sacrificial Lamb of God, through whose blood we have God's eternal life. John is indeed the herald of Jesus; and for speaking the truth to power, King Herod, John was imprisoned and executed.

John's example challenges us to be heralds of Jesus in our families, our workplaces, and our communities by the way we live.

The author of the gospel summed up John's mission in the canticle or song of Zechariah, John's father. "For you will go before the Lord to prepare his ways." We too are called to prepare the way of the Lord so the Lord can enter the hearts of our fellow human beings, so that through our own hearts the grace and favor of God can empower others to "do what is right, love goodness and walk humbly with your God."

And there's no better place to begin than in our own families.

But how do we prepare the way for the Lord in our families? Here is an approach.

First, continue to create a better sense of togetherness, a feeling of closeness and care for one another. Keep in touch with one another, even if it's only by telephone, e-mail, or Skype; be hospitable, checking in with elderly relatives. Remember birthdays and anniversaries, and celebrate them together, if possible. Participate in special family events— for example, graduations, baptisms, confirmations, marriages, cookouts, Sunday liturgies, and so forth. Communicate, take responsibility for family chores, spend time with one another; share the good news as well as the bad; keep your word and thereby build up trust.

Second, take control of family life. There are so many activities that can easily divide a family—activities all valuable in themselves—but if not checked, they can rob families of time together.

And finally, parents must let their sons or daughters become the persons God created them to be. The purpose of family is to nurture children in a secure and loving environment until they become mature enough to venture out on their own and become responsible persons. Parents let go of them so they can take their place in the world as responsible adults.

So, as we enter summer, like John the Baptizer, prepare the way for the Lord to enter your families, workplaces, and communities wherever you are.

Fourteenth Sunday
in Ordinary Time

I don't know about you, but I can't keep up with technology. Here's an e-mail from a daughter to her father.

> Dearest Dad, I am coming home to get married soon, so get your checkbook out. As you know, I am in Australia … and he lives in Scotland. We met on a dating website, became friends on Facebook and had long chats on Whatsapp. He proposed to me on Skype. My beloved Dad, I need your blessing, good wishes, and a big wedding. Lots of love and thanks. Your favorite daughter, Lilly.

And here's her dad's response.

> My Dear Lilly, Wow! Really? I suggest you get married on Twitter, have fun on Tango, buy kids on Amazon, and pay for it all through PayPal. And when you get fed up with this husband, sell him on eBay. Love, Dad.

As I said, I simply can't keep up with these tech applications.

Many of you have read or seen T. S. Eliot's play *Murder in the Cathedral*. The play dramatizes the martyrdom of Thomas Becket, the twelfth-century Archbishop of Canterbury. Becket challenged King Henry II's unfair policies. The King shouts, "Will not someone rid me of this troublesome priest." Four knights descend on the cathedral to kill Becket. Three priests pull Becket back into the cathedral to save him. They bar the cathedral door, but Becket shouts out, "Unbar the door. Throw open the door."

Like Becket, Jesus demands that we open the doors of our hearts to God and to our fellow human beings. Yes, open our hearts to God in prayer and open our hearts to one another. How? By being generous; by forgiving those who have wronged us; and by caring for family, neighbors, and colleagues. Isn't that why we gather here today? To open our hearts?

The word of God takes us back in our imaginations to the sixth century before Jesus. Ancient Babylonia conquered Israel, leveled Jerusalem to the ground, and deported many. And yet amid this catastrophe, Zechariah spoke about the future, about a messianic king who will usher in a new era of peace, justice, and prosperity (Zec 9:9–10).

Zechariah's words challenge us to always hope in God.

A modern French philosopher, Paul Ricoeur, argues that hope is a fundamental characteristic of human life. Think about it. Right now, you may be hoping I will stop talking so you can get on with your chores.

In his letter to the Christian community at Rome, Paul spoke about the Spirit of God dwelling within us. We are living temples of God. The Spirit within us empowers us to live lives of honesty, responsibility, integrity, courage, compassion, and faith in God (Rom 8:9, 11–13).

In the Gospel according to Matthew, Jesus began with a prayer of praise. Yes, Jesus is uniquely one with his heavenly Father. And then Jesus invited us to enter this life. "Come to me, all you who find life burdensome and I will refresh you" (Mt 11:25–30). Yes, when we begin to think that our lives are empty or burdensome, Jesus is there to fill our emptiness, to lighten our burdens, whether they are broken relationships, illness, the death of a loved one, the loss of a job, or whatever.

Today, I would like to reflect on Jesus as "our true wisdom who guides us, brings us good news and provides for us" in light of his invitation, "Come to me, all you who find life burdensome and I will refresh you."

Lawrence of Arabia was one of the most successful films of all time. Much of the story is drawn from T. E. Lawrence, a British archaeological scholar and military strategist (colonel by age thirty) known for his activities in World War I. Lawrence's memoir, written in 1926, is titled *The Seven Pillars of Wisdom*. I would guess Lawrence had in mind the book of Proverbs (9:1) in the wisdom literature of ancient Israel. "*Wisdom* has built her house; she has set up her *seven columns*" (emphasis mine). In scripture, the number seven is often used to represent completion or perfection.

Jesus is our true wisdom, the image of the God we cannot see, our guide, our good news, and our provider.

First, Jesus as our wisdom gives all the guidance we need. We have the Spirit dwelling within us. We are "led by the Spirit of God" (Rom 8:14). And God has bestowed the gifts of the Spirit on us. These are wisdom (to recognize what truly matters in life), intelligence (to discern what's true), courage (to stand up for what's right), empathy or compassion (to care for the needy), good judgment (to do the right thing), and wonder and awe (to worship the great God of this universe). Yes, Jesus will provide all the guidance we need.

Second, in a world that desperately needs good news, Jesus has provided us with that. The word *gospel* means "good news." The good news is about Jesus, his death and resurrection (Acts 17:18). All we need is in Jesus.

Words can be powerful and life changing. The good news of Jesus is dynamically relevant to all generations, cultures, and situations. People's needs are always the same. The message of the gospel is always the same. Study the good news. Set aside regular time to meditate on the scriptures, the privileged expression of our faith.

Lastly, Jesus taught us to pray. "Give us this day our daily bread" (Mt 6:11).

Look to Jesus. He will provide us with all we need.

One of my favorite biblical narratives is the story of Elijah. The New Testament tells us that Elijah was a human being "like us." And yet "he prayed earnestly that it might not rain, and for three years and six months it did not rain upon the land. Then he prayed again, and the sky gave rain, and the earth produced its fruits" (Jas 5:17–18).

Elijah trusted in God's providence, God's care for us. When the brook that provided water for Elijah dried up, God sent Elijah to a *widow* for food. The point is, when one door closes, God is about to open another door in our lives. Elijah asked for food. The widow replied that she and her son were about to eat their last meal and die. But Elijah promised that if she was generous, God would provide for her needs. He said, "The jar of flour shall not go empty, nor the jug of oil run dry, until the day when the Lord sends rain upon the earth" (1 Kgs 17:14).

The widow did exactly as Elijah asked. And it turned out exactly so. This woman of great faith was prepared to give all she had. And God supplied her needs. The point is, if we give generously, we will discover that we cannot out-give God. God will do amazing things for and through us. This doesn't mean life will be easy. The widow's son died; yet amazingly Elijah was able to pick the boy up and give him back to his mother saying, "See, your son is alive!" (1 Kgs 17:24).

Yes, Jesus is indeed our wisdom who guides us, brings us good news, and provides for us so we can become our better selves: images of God.

FIFTEENTH SUNDAY IN
ORDINARY TIME

During these summer days, here are a few thoughts worth considering. In a farming community, all the townspeople gathered in church to pray for rain. But only one person brought an umbrella. That's faith.

We go to bed without assurance of tomorrow, but still we set the alarm clock. That's hope.

We see suffering everywhere, but we still get married and raise children. That's love.

We plan big things despite zero knowledge of the future. That's confidence.

Finally, on a man's shirt was written, "I am not 80 years old; I am sweet 16 with 64 years of experience." That's attitude. Yes, here are a few thoughts worth mulling over.

The word of God takes us back to a prophet known as Second Isaiah in the sixth century before Jesus. The author was fascinated with the awe, wonder. and grandeur of this universe. And he proclaimed that, just as the spring rains and winter snows bring forth new life on the ground, so too does the word of God bring forth goodness. And why? Because God's word is life giving and will ultimately achieve what God has set out to do (Isa 55:10–11).

Today we pray, "Thy will be done" even though at times God's seems to be the opposite of what we want to happen. Yes, God's word ultimately will achieve its purpose despite the hindrances we place before it.

Paul urged the Christian community in the Rome of the 60s, who were undergoing hardships, to stay the course and not lose their confidence in God. Paul went on to say that just as a mother in her labor brings forth a beautiful child, so God ultimately will reveal his glory and splendor and grandeur despite the human tragedies and natural disasters we encounter daily (Rom 8:18–23).

This passage should inspire us to have confidence in God, especially when we may begin to think that, to quote the Irish poet William Butler Yeats,

> Things fall apart; the center cannot hold;
> mere anarchy is loosed upon the world, the blood dimm'd
> tide is loosed" ("The Second Coming").

One day we feel healthy; the next day we discover we face a life-threatening disease. Paul's words challenge us to remember our ultimate purpose: eternal life with God.

In the Gospel according to Matthew, Jesus spoke to us in a parable about a sower or, even better, different kinds of soil. The sower is God.

Notice how generous God is. He spreads his goodness everywhere. The seed is the word of God. The different kinds of soil are different people. Some people are like rocky ground—initially enthusiastic but so shallow in their spirituality that they forget God when the going gets tough. Others are like thorny ground; they let the cares of this earthly life, so consume them that they become unaware of their purpose in life: to live in relationship with God.

Still other people are like good soil; they not only hear God's word but do it. Jesus asks us, Who are we in this parable? Good soil! Yes, the word of God gives us much to think about—in Isaiah, the power of God's word (it ultimately achieves what it sets out to do); in Paul, hope or confidence amid hardship; and in Matthew, receptivity to the word of God as a disciple of Jesus (Mt 13:1–23).

We might ask, in light of Paul's advice to the community in Rome, "How do we cope with the challenges of life?"

President John F. Kennedy said, "The new frontier of which I speak is not a set of promises—it is a set of challenges. It sums up not what I intend to offer the American people, but what I intend to ask of them."

Life includes challenges, problems, and hassles. We sometimes imagine that if we could just deal with the immediate challenges we're facing, all our problems would vanish. But life isn't like that. If we resolve one problem, others are just around the corner.

The temptation is to see this truth as preventing us from doing the right thing. Not so! The Bible is true to life. Look at what so many people today face around the world—for example, in Syria and Iraq, the South Sudan, and the Congo.

How should you cope with the challenges of life? First, talk to God as you would with a friend. Whatever situations you may face, bring them to God in prayer.

Second, trust that God is in control. Faith means trusting God's unconditional love for us. "Faith," C. S. Lewis wrote, "is the art of holding on to things … once accepted, in spite of your changing moods." Yes, it's hard to trust when everything seems to be going wrong.

But think, for example, about St. Paul. This leader of the early church was at one time locked away, imprisoned, apparently unable to do what he was called to do—to proclaim the "good news." Jesus Christ lives. And because he lives, we live in God.

For Paul, amid all these challenges, it must have been very hard to see what good might possibly come out of all the dishonesty, delays, and dithering he encountered as he faced a trial on trumped-up charges. Read about it in Acts 24–26. Yet, as Paul wrote, "We know that in all things God works for the good of those who love him" (Rom 8:28).

Paul's imprisonment resulted in his being sent to Rome to preach the gospel, precisely what he wanted to do. Two thousand years later, vast numbers of innocent people, undergoing inescapable hardships, have been inspired by Paul's story about how good came out of evil.

You and I may never know in this life how God uses our faithfulness to achieve his purposes. Perhaps our prayer should be, "Lord, thank you that you are with us. Thank you that through all these problems, challenges, and hassles of life, you work for the good of those who love you."

Take every opportunity God gives us never to give up on doing the right thing. Whatever challenges we're facing, keep praying, keep trusting, keep looking for opportunities to serve God; and never, ever give up. Pray, as we face challenges, that God will give us the grace to persevere and carry through on doing the right thing.

I close with this thought: How about forgiving those we don't want to forgive, being compassionate to those we instinctively want to punish, making peace with those who have badly injured us, caring for those we know need us, persevering in what we know we should do when we want to give up, carrying our inescapable crosses when we would rather get rid of them, and loving when the last thing we want to do is love.

We have the potential to do great things for God. Begin with ordinary things. Pray that the word of God will inspire us to see Jesus more clearly in our lives, to love him more dearly, and to follow him more nearly.

Sixteenth Sunday in Ordinary Time

You may have heard about the fellow who was in a bar, staring at his drink, when a troublemaker grabbed the drink and gulped it down.

The fellow burst into tears. "Oh, come on," said the troublemaker. "I didn't think you'd cry."

The fellow said, "This is the worst day of my life. My boss fired me. My car was stolen. Then I left my wallet on the bus. And at home, my dog bit me. I came to this bar to put an end to it all. I dropped a capsule into my drink and was watching the poison dissolve; and then you showed up and drank it! But enough about me. How's your day?"

The troublemaker was about to have a bad day.

The word of God takes us back to the wisdom literature attributed to Solomon and collected into a series of biblical books in the second century before Jesus (Wis 12:13, 16–19).

Don't we wish we always had the wisdom to distinguish what's really important? Life isn't simply a matter of acquiring and spending. No! Our faith proclaims that our ultimate purpose is to live in a relationship with God forever. That is why St. Paul urged us to "think of what is above, not of what is on earth" (Col 3:2).

Reinhold Niebuhr, a twentieth-century theologian, captured a nugget of wisdom in his "Serenity Prayer."

> God, give us the grace to accept with serenity the things that cannot be changed, courage to change the things which should be changed, and the wisdom to distinguish the one from the other. Living one day at a time … Trusting that You, God, will make all things right, if I surrender to Your will.

Today's reading was written to inspire Jews undergoing hardships to persevere in their fidelity to God's covenant. God, the author said, is a patient judge. He is mighty and powerful, the source of all good. And for such a mighty, caring, and forgiving God, the author proclaimed, we should be grateful.

The author may prompt us to describe our own image of God. The Bible gives many splendid images. A walking companion, a God as tender as a mother. The image of God in the parables of the good shepherd and the prodigal son is balanced with the image of the last judgment. All these splendid images cannot fully capture the inexhaustible reality of God. So, what are our images of God?

In his letter to the Christian community at Rome, Paul spoke about the Spirit or energy of God dwelling within us. When we pray, for example, "Come, Holy Spirit," we are praying for a greatly increased sense of that presence of God in us. God, of course, is present everywhere, yet we don't always sense it (Rom 8:26–27).

Paul asked us to be aware of the presence of the Spirit in our daily lives. After all, we are "living temples of God." We might pray, as Paul and Barnabas did in the book of Acts 13, that God will give us the courage to speak the "good news" boldly.

In the Gospel according to Matthew, Jesus told the parable of the wheat and the weeds. Good and evil, sin and virtue, live together. And yes, God is patient, tolerating evil alongside good. But the harvest will come when we will be accountable for our attitudes and behavior. In that judgment, we will clearly see our true self from our false one. Jesus proclaimed loudly that good will triumph, even if here and now it seems evil may be overcoming good (Mt 13:24–43).

One of the biggest obstacles to faith in God is the suffering of the innocent. The book of Job attempted to grapple with the problem. If there is a God who loves us, how come there is so much suffering in the world, so much injustice and violence?

There are no easy answers. Yet God meets us amid our struggles. In fact, people who have gone through the greatest suffering often have strong faith. They testify to the presence of God within, strengthening and comforting them amid pain.

In her book *The Hiding Place*, Corrie ten Boom describes how her sister, dying in a concentration camp, said, "We must tell them that there is no pit so deep that God is not deeper still. They will listen to us, Corrie, because we have been there." These sisters trusted in God despite the ugliness they had witnessed.

How do we respond to injustice? The biblical psalmist trusted that God ultimately would put things right; he recognized that God's got the whole world in his hands. It is a great blessing to live under a system of justice. It is a terrible ordeal to live under a corrupt system. But ultimately, God will call us to account. In the meantime, we are called to do everything within our power to see that the right thing is done.

It is relatively easy to trust in God when everything is going well in our lives. However, there are times when we face major challenges to our faith. Among his many trials, St. Paul, for example, was shipwrecked three times. In one scene (Ac 27:13 and following), a hurricane appeared. Luke wrote that they finally gave up all hope of being saved. Yet Paul kept on trusting in God, telling those on board that God was still in control. Extraordinarily, Paul, the prisoner, stopped the sailors from jumping ship.

The crisis gave Paul an opportunity to speak about his faith. He knew God wanted the very best for him, as he does for us. Paul assured them, "Not a hair of the head of any one of you will be lost" (Acts 27:34). And "when he said this, he took bread, gave thanks to God in front of them all, broke it, and began to eat ... and they took some food themselves. All reached shore safely."

Paul surely must have prayed, "Lord, thank you that you protect me even when disaster strikes. When things go wrong, help me not to be afraid but rather to keep up my courage and to have faith in you."

Today, regardless of whatever challenges we are facing, let's put our trust in God, believing that God will be with us in whatever God asks us to do. I close with a few lines from a favorite prayer of Thomas Merton.

> My Lord God,
> … I trust you always though
> I may seem to be lost and in the shadow of death.
> I will not fear, for you are ever with me,
> and you will never leave me to face my perils alone.

SEVENTEENTH SUNDAY
IN ORDINARY TIME

I once enjoyed air travel; now it seems like a hassle. First, either I'm getting bigger, or the seats are getting smaller. Have you had that experience?

I miss the intercom humor of airline personnel in the good old days. For example, I remember a captain saying, "Folks, we've reached cruising altitude. I'm turning off the seat belt sign and switching to autopilot so I can chat with all of you for the rest of the flight." Or, "We have now reached our cruising altitude. Please feel free to move about the aircraft, but please stay inside the plane until we land. It's a bit cold outside, and if you walk on the wings, it affects the flight pattern." Or, "There may be fifty ways to leave your lover, but there are only four ways out of this airplane." I say, bring back the humor of the good old days.

The word of God carries us back to King Solomon in the tenth century before Jesus. He gave ancient Israel a brief touch of splendor. The Bible tells us very little about Solomon compared with his father David. But it does tell us this: Solomon probably was twelve or fourteen years old when he came to the throne. He was clever with affairs of state, built a splendid temple in Jerusalem, married many wives, owned four thousand chariot horses, uttered three thousand proverbs, and wrote more than a thousand songs. Wow! These are mighty accomplishments.

In today's passage, God appeared in a dream to Solomon. "Ask me for something and I will give it to you." Surprisingly Solomon didn't ask for power, wealth, or health. No, he asked only for the wisdom to know the right thing to do (1 Kgs 3:5, 7–12).

Think about it. What would we ask of God? I confess that I might ask for a winning Powerball ticket. How about you?

Making right choices is really the stuff of life. Should I go to this school or that, take this job, or the other? Many of us think hard about our choices, trying to make the best ones for ourselves and our families, who rely on the wisdom of our decisions. Often we must choose between right and wrong, greed and generosity, honesty and lies, people and things. And occasionally, we may need to choose between life and death—for example, whether to continue a loved one on medical life support. In all decisions, small and great, that affect work, career, family, and social life, even leisure time, we pray to God for the wisdom to do the right thing.

In his letter to the Christian community in Rome, Paul wrote, "All things work for the good for those who love God." But in light of media news day after day, we might surmise all things aren't working for the good. But Paul, the incredibly faith-filled disciple of Jesus, who trusted in God and God's presence in his own life, especially as he encountered hardships of one kind or the other in his ministry, urged us to fix our eyes on the ultimate prize—eternal life in relationship with God. God, Paul proclaimed, will ultimately transform us into a new kind of spiritual embodiment just as God had already transformed the earthly Jesus into a new heavenly reality (Rom 8:28–30).

Paul's words may be asking whether we're fixing our eyes on the ultimate prize, looking beyond this earthly horizon to the heavenly horizon.

In the Gospel according to Matthew, Jesus continued the theme of choices, as in the first reading. In the first parable, a farmer plowing someone else's field hits a clump that turns out to be a buried treasure. He thinks, "Finders keepers." He sells everything he has to buy the field so he can claim the treasure as his own. In the second parable, we have a merchant who is like the treasure hunters in our own time. They spend their entire lives searching for more riches that will guarantee them happiness. Here, the merchant finds a pearl so magnificent that he sells all the riches he has accumulated in life to buy it (Mt 13:44–52).

Jesus says to us in these parables, carpe diem, seize the moment. Make the right decision. "Seek first the kingdom of God and his righteousness, and all these things will be given you besides." (Mt 6:33) So much for making right decisions.

But what about the decision maker? Solomon, for example, despite his mighty accomplishments, seemed to have character flaws. He countenanced non-Israelite religious practices, launched expensive building projects, imposed high taxes to pay for them, and conscripted work gangs to build them. As a result, his policies created widespread discontent that ultimately split the kingdom into two after his death. (1 Kgs)

Right decisions presuppose men and women with character or integrity. Character defines who we are at the core of our inmost self. It's an ethical reality. Centuries ago the Hebrew psalmist spoke of King David as a great (though imperfect) leader who guided his people with integrity of heart and skillful hands (Ps 78:72).

But leadership requires not only character or integrity but courage. Whether it's starting a new business, battling a life-threatening disease, getting married, or struggling to overcome an addiction, life demands courage to move beyond our fears and self-doubts to achieve something worthwhile.

The most common phrase in the New Testament is "Do not be afraid." The most common phrase in the Old Testament is "Be not afraid." When the phrase appears more than a thousand times in both testaments, God may be trying to get a message across to us.

Finally, leaders have a can-do attitude. They know what they want, why they want it, and how to communicate what they want to others so they can galvanize them into action. They're optimists, they get the facts, they're enthusiastic and self-confident, and their confidence instills confidence in others. At different times in life, all of us are called to be leaders—as professionals, businesspeople, parents, citizens in a community, and volunteers in an organization. But in the final analysis, you may ask, What is the most important ingredient of leadership? Character. Courage. A can-do attitude. Here's how one American hero put it to the cadets at West Point:

> Your character, that's what's important in leadership. I
> tell cynics who scoff at character to go out and look at
> the leadership failures … in this country in the last 100
> years. (They) were not failures in competence; they were
> failures in character. Greed, lying, prejudice, racism,
> intolerance, sexism, hate, immorality, amorality—none
> of these things are competence failures. They are all
> character failures. You see, leadership involves things
> like ethics … a sense of duty … a value system …
> morality … integrity. And that is why character is what
> counts in leadership. Integrity: that is the linchpin in
> all of this.

If you want to be inspired by a list of wonderful virtues, I suggest we might want to start with Rudyard's Kipling's poem "If."

Yes, always seek the right thing to do—not what is fashionable, not what is merely acceptable but what's right. And having found what's right, as the slogan says, "just do it."

TRANSFIGURATION OF THE LORD

I recently spoke to a group, and afterward a friend rushed up and said with enthusiasm, "I really enjoyed your talk; will it be published?"

With tongue in cheek, I said, "Yes, I hope to publish it posthumously."

"Good," said the friend, "the sooner the better."

It's back-to-school time. How many parents are excited?

Now, I'm going to give you a two-part quiz. Here's part one:

- Name the last two movies to win the Oscar for best picture.
- Who were the last two teams to win the Super Bowl?
- Name the two wealthiest people in the world (according to the latest issue of *Forbes Magazine*).

I don't know about you, but I didn't get 100 percent.

Now try part two of the quiz:

- Think of two teachers who made a difference for the better in your life.
- Name two friends who helped you through a difficult time.
- Identify two mentors or coaches who taught you something worthwhile.

I bet you named two people in all three categories.

The point I want to make is simple: we quickly forget headlines.

However, we become "heroes and heroines" when we make a difference for the better in people's lives, when we help them through challenges, and when we affirm purpose or meaning in their lives.

That, my friends, is precisely what Jesus does. Yes, Jesus is a rabbi or teacher who shows us purpose in life and how to live in relationship with God; a friend whom we always can trust and who is always with us, especially as we face challenges; and a mentor who inspires us to become the best version of ourselves.

Now what does the word of God have to say to us? The book of Daniel is about a legendary hero who interpreted dreams, survived a burning furnace, and escaped a lion's den. Here the author described in apocalyptic or "fiery" imagery a mysterious figure who was like a Son of man. He went before the throne of God, the ancient One, who entrusted him with the universe. As we read on, the author urged his fellow persecuted Jews in the second century before Jesus to continue in fidelity to God's covenant, even if it meant martyrdom, because in the resurrection, they would "shine like the stars." Stop worrying, the author pleaded. Trust in God who controls the universe. Good advice! (Dn 7:9–10, 13–14).

The author of the second letter of Peter alluded to the final coming of the living Christ. The disciples were eyewitnesses to the transfiguration. They saw the glory of God in the earthly Jesus; they heard God's voice affirm his identity. The living Christ will come again like a light out of darkness, like the dawn of a new day (2 Pt 1:16–19).

He is the revelation of God to us. In other words, everything God ever wanted to do for or say to us he already did and said in the living Christ; that's why John said he is our way, our truth, and our life.

The author of the Gospel according to Matthew spoke about a mountain and a cloud. Mountains symbolize the human ascent to God and clouds, God's descent on us. Here Jesus appeared on Mount Tabor as a dazzling figure, whose face was like the sun and whose clothes were as white as light. Peter, James, and John saw Jesus's inner identity as Son of God burst through his outer earthly appearance. And the voice said, "Listen to him" (Mt 17:1–9).

Who is this Jesus, this God-man? And why listen to him?

Jesus, the Gospels tell us, was a real historical person, flesh and blood like ourselves. He was a rabbi, a teacher, a prophet who proclaimed the in-breaking or initiation of the kingdom of God. He worked signs and wonders; possessed authority to forgive; was one with the God of Israel; and was crucified, died, and was raised up. Yes, Jesus Christ is alive. And because he lives, we live. That is the good news.

This living Christ invites us, so says John 15:15, to be "friends, because I have told you everything I have heard from my Father."

But what is a friend? I recently came across a survey of eight hundred people born between 1981 and the early 2000s, the so-called millennials. The results gave a snapshot of a lonely generation. More people live alone today than at any other point in our recorded history. This survey found that people had a very large number of Facebook friends but still felt a sense of loneliness.

Social media, of course, is no substitute for real, face-to-face friendships. After all Genesis 2–3 says we were created for friendship with God and one another.

The Bible, of course, is very realistic about friendships. We see examples of relationships at their best and at their worst. For me, friendships include at least three ingredients.

First, they include partnerships. All of us need good partnerships. Perhaps that's why Jesus sent his disciples out two by two. Value our partnerships.

Second, nurture our friendships. From the beginning of Christianity, we see examples of friends working together in partnership. Paul and Barnabas, for example, were partners in proclaiming the "good news." They "dedicated their lives ... to Jesus Christ." But as we read on in the book of Acts, we see that they had a "sharp disagreement" and parted company. But in the providence of God, everything worked out well in the end. Barnabas found a new partner in Mark. Paul found a new partner in Silas, and they "went through Syria and Cilicia, bringing strength to the churches" there (Acts 15).

Obviously, we want to do our best to resolve differences and avoid painful parting. But the point is, we should nurture our friendships. Martin Luther King Jr. gave some good advice about how to nurture friendships. "Forgiveness is not an occasional act; it is a permanent attitude" in our friendships with one another.

Finally, make loyalty a priority. If we sow loyalty, we will reap loyalty. Be loyal, even when friends aren't in our company. We will become trustworthy among those who aren't our friends.

Yes, friendships value and nurture our partnerships and make loyalty a priority. Above all, think of Jesus as our best friend and soul mate and confidant, especially in prayer. Jesus calls us friends because he has told us everything he has heard from his Father. Value that relationship, nurture it especially in prayer, and make loyalty or fidelity a priority.

St. Paul gave us excellent advice. "Do not neglect to do good and to share what you have; God is pleased by sacrifices of that kind" (Heb 13:16).

Perhaps our prayer might be, Lord, pour out your Spirit upon us. Help us to work together in our partnerships so that we can bring "good news" to one another. Nurture our friendships, especially with you, and help us with your grace to stay loyal to our friendships so we can keep on doing all the good we can, by all the means we can, in all the ways we can, in all the places we can, at all the times we can, for all the people we can, as long as ever we can. Amen.

Nineteenth Sunday in Ordinary Time

I read about a man who suffered an apparent heart attack while shopping. Paramedics rushed him to the hospital, where he had an emergency bypass. When he woke from surgery, a hospital staff person appeared at his bedside and asked how he would like to pay. "Do you have health insurance?" she asked.

"No."

"Perhaps family or relatives might help you with payments."

The patient said, "I only have a spinster aunt, and she is a nun."

The staffer noted, "Nuns are not spinsters. They're married to God."

The patient replied, "Okay. Send the bill to my uncle." Now that's a novel interpretation of affordable health care.

The word of God describes the ninth century before Jesus (the 800s). Here the main character is Elijah, who did "wonderful things for God and his people." He was a rainmaker who ended a scorching drought, saving many lives. He preached fidelity to God's covenant. For denouncing royal wrongdoings, Queen Jezebel ran Elijah out of town, so to speak. The once-mighty Elijah now hid in a cave, trying to determine where to go next. He cried out, "Where is God now?" He was depressed. He looked but didn't find God in extraordinary phenomena: in a tornado, an earthquake, or a fire. Instead, he found God in an ordinary "tiny, whispering sound." Elijah, ready to give up on life, found

God where he least expected to find him. That fact reenergized Elijah (1 Kgs 19:9, 11–13).

Perhaps we've asked a similar question ourselves. Where is God now? What about the sudden death of a spouse or child? An unexpected divorce? A life-threatening sickness? A job promotion that went to someone else? A vacation that turned into two rainy weeks? A business deal that went wrong? In such challenges, it's easy to wonder where God is and forget Jesus's words. "Do not be afraid, I am always with you."

In his letter to the Christian community at Rome. Paul grieved that his fellow Jews didn't see in Jesus the fulfillment of their hopes. If only he could bridge Judaism and Christianity! Paul waxed eloquently about what God had done for the Hebrews. He entered a covenant with them centuries before and promised a Messiah, whom his fellow Jews didn't recognize when he did come in Jesus. Yes, for Paul, Jesus was the fulfillment and foundation of all our hopes. He is the face of God among us (Rom 9:1–5).

In the Gospel according to Matthew, Jesus had an extraordinary day of feeding more than five thousand people. He then went off to converse with his heavenly Father in prayer, while his disciples set sail only to be awakened in the middle of the night by a raging storm on the sea of Galilee. Suddenly, what they first thought was a ghost turned out to be Jesus. "It is I; do not be afraid," Jesus said. Jesus bid Peter, "Come."

Peter, fearful he may drown, cried out, "Lord, save me." In this crisis Peter lost trust in Jesus. Back in the boat with Jesus, the disciples calmed down, acknowledging that Jesus was truly the Son of God. The gospel invites us to keep our eyes fixed on Jesus, and if we do, our faith will conquer our fears (Mt 14:22–33).

Two gospel phrases caught my eye, and I simply would paraphrase them into, "Help me, Lord!" and "Do not be afraid; God is with me."

One of the most common prayers in the Bible is "Help." It's a simple prayer we can pray every day in any situation. For example, "Help me, Lord, in broken relationships." Perhaps we're struggling with a relationship—in our workplace, community, marriage, or close friend. However bad our situation may seem, we always can make Psalm 88 our prayer. "I cry to you for help, O Lord."

Help us, Lord, in our struggles with sin. Do we ever find ourselves trapped in addictions or bad habits, sins we want to break free from? St. Paul wrote centuries ago, "What I do, I do not understand. For I do not do what I want but I do what I hate" (Rom 7:15).

Paul went on to say he needed God's help. He cried out, "Who will deliver me from this mortal body?" (Rom 7:24). And then he answered, "Thanks be to God through Jesus Christ our Lord." John Newton, the eighteenth-century British sailor, preacher, and author of "Amazing Grace" put it well: "I'm not what I want to be. I'm not what I ought to be. I'm not what I one day will be. But thank God I'm not what I once was." Yes, the Spirit of God dwelling within us will help us live the kind of life we know God wants us to live.

The second paraphrase is, do not be afraid; God is with us. "God with us" (Emmanuel) is one of the titles the New Testament uses for Jesus (Mt 1:23). That the God who created the universe should be with us is an extraordinary promise. To experience "God with us" is life changing. Realizing the awesome indwelling of God energizes us. God through the death and resurrection of Jesus by the power of the Spirit has reestablished our relationship with God, since at the beginning of creation, as the author of Genesis said, God created us in the divine image.

God actually dwells in us. St. Paul asked, "Do you not know that you are the temple of God, and that the Spirit of God dwells in you?" (1 Cor 3:16). In the life-giving waters of baptism, God has gifted us with his life and Spirit. We possess the gifts of the Spirit within ourselves to guide us. These gifts are wisdom (to recognize what truly matters in life), intelligence (to discern what's true), courage, empathy or compassion, good judgment, and wonder and awe (to worship the great God of this universe).

God is amazing. "Eye has not seen, and ear has not heard ... what God has prepared for those who love him" (1 Cor 2:9). "At present we see indistinctly, as in a mirror, but then face to face" (1 Cor 13:12).

God is with us. In difficult times, listen to God's promises over our feelings and emotions. The psalmist says God will be with us in our troubles (Ps 91). But God doesn't promise a trouble-free life. Rather, he promises that he will be with us in our troubles.

God's also with us in our successes. Have you ever been disappointed when someone else was given the privilege of doing something you wanted to do? Rather than being disappointed, bless the efforts of others and pray for them that they will keep following the Lord in all they do. Remember, life may not be easy, but Jesus promised that if we stay close to him, we will bear much fruit (Jn 15).

Today, we might ponder those phrases in the gospel: "Lord, save me" and "Take courage, it is I; do not be afraid." Help me, Lord. And may I always remember not to be afraid. For you, God, are always with me—in my struggles and my successes.

Twentieth Sunday in Ordinary Time

Some baseball fans are passionate about their teams. A *New York Post* story covered two youngsters playing in Central Park. A big dog suddenly attacked them. Thinking quickly, the older boy grabbed some rope and lassoed the dog. A reporter ran over and began to write, "Yankees Fan Saves Friend from Vicious Dog." "I'm not a Yankees fan," the boy noted. So the reporter said, "Mets Fan Rescues Friend." "I don't like the Mets," the boy said. The reporter asked, "What team do you root for?" "The Red Sox." The reporter then wrote, "Ruthless Child Almost Chokes to Death Beloved Pet." Moral: don't say you're a Red Sox fan in New York.

The word of God carries us back to the sixth century before Jesus (the 500s). Salvation, the author proclaimed, is for all people who try their best to do the right thing. This truth shocked many Jews who thought salvation was exclusively theirs. The author challenged us to treat one another fairly and compassionately, because all of us are made in the image of God, so wrote the author of Genesis (Isa 56:1, 6–7).

In today's letter Paul spoke about his successful ministry to the Gentile Christians. Through Jesus's dying and rising, all people are called to be in relationship with God forever. Paul prayed that his fellow Jews, God's special people, would see in Jesus their promised Messiah. Paul here may have wondered, What kind of missionary disciples are we? (Rom 11:13–15, 29–32).

In the Gospel according to Matthew, an assertive mother from Canaan sought out Jesus. She wanted her daughter healed and would do whatever it took. This Gentile woman begged Jesus to heal her demon-afflicted daughter. At first Jesus seemed to treat this mother harshly. Then there was a startling turnaround. The mother uttered a prayer: "Lord, help me." Jesus replied, "Woman, great is your faith. Let it be done for you as you wish." And the daughter was healed (Mt 15:21–28).

This faith-filled woman segued easily into the heroes and heroines in Christianity who can guide or coach us about the spiritual life and fundamental questions, such as, "What is my purpose in life?"

In their hearts, people yearn for something or someone beyond themselves who can give purpose or meaning to their lives. This longing can be satisfied in a variety of ways—through a family or profession, a commitment to a cause such as Habitat for Humanity, and so forth. When people find something that gives transcendent meaning to their lives, that purpose awakens new energies. They become believers.

We are by nature believers. To be human is to live by faith. Think about the ordinary things we do. We sit in the church pew; we don't expect it to collapse.

St. Augustine, whose feast day we celebrate in August, is one of many faith heroes in Christianity, a guide for us in the spiritual life. After many detours in his life, Augustine found his purpose. He wrote, "God, you have made us for yourself, and our hearts are restless until they rest in you." In other words, no matter who we are, our true purpose is to be in relationship with God.

So, who is Augustine? He was born in the middle of fourth-century Africa (modern-day Algeria). The Roman Empire in the west was descending into chaos during his lifetime and finally collapsed in 476.

Although Augustine authored numerous writings, he's known for two classics, *Confessions* and *City of God*.

Confessions is a spiritual autobiography, his dialogue with God. *City of God* is his interpretation of the church, a community of saints and scoundrels, on a pilgrimage to the heavenly city of God. It's worthwhile reading.

Augustine symbolizes the search for God in one's own life; he passionately sought the truth. His *Confessions* is as relevant today for people adrift as Thomas Merton's *Seven-Story Mountain*. Both searched for true purpose in life.

Monica, Augustine's mother and a devout Christian, did her best to educate her catechumenate son in the essentials. But he drifted away from Christianity when he began his studies in Carthage. He excelled in rhetoric, the art of argumentation; and dabbled in fashionable philosophies. He soon became a famous teacher of rhetoric.

He also fathered a child out of wedlock and lived with a mistress. One of Augustine's memorable quotations is, "God, give me chastity, but not yet."

A question that haunted Augustine throughout his adult life was the problem of evil. How can there be an all-good God when there's such incredible human suffering. Eventually Augustine met Ambrose, bishop of Milan in Italy, whose persuasive homilies led Augustine to focus on the direction of his life. Augustine described his conversion graphically in the *Confessions*. He went into his garden and just sat there. He heard a voice saying, "Take and read, take and read." So Augustine picked up the Bible. And in his autobiography, he wrote, "I seized, opened, and in silence read that section on which my eyes first fell: 'conduct ourselves properly as in the day, not in orgies and drunkenness, not in promiscuity and licentiousness, not in rivalry and jealousy. But put on the Lord Jesus Christ …' No further would I read … for instantly at the end of the sentence, by a light, as it were … all the darkness of doubt vanished away." Augustine found his true purpose in life in that conversion moment.

From that moment on, he became a passionate disciple, a major intellectual, spiritual, and cultural icon in the Christian tradition. After Ambrose baptized him, Augustine went back to Africa and founded a monastic community. But soon, acclaimed bishop Augustine became a prolific author. He refuted the basic falsehoods that plagued Christianity. The universe, the work of God, he argued, is essentially good; and a provident God guides this universe to the fullness of the kingdom. The church or community of disciples is holy but is made up of saints and sinners. Above all, human beings need God's grace to live the kind of life God wants them to live.

Augustine acknowledged that there's something not quite right with human beings. Some people choose evil over good, wrong over right, falsehood over truth. Why? Because there's a tendency or pull within them to sometimes choose their worse rather than their better selves. He called this "original sin." Human beings had fallen from grace and cry out for salvation.

Augustine looked beyond the world of things to an all-good God who became "one of us" in Jesus and is alive by the power of the Spirit in human beings. By God's grace, Augustine argued, human beings are in relationship with God. But they must continually struggle against a tendency within themselves to choose wrong over right.

The words of Augustine, a spiritual guide, a faith hero like the Canaanite woman, challenge us to focus on the quality of our lives and our souls' destinies. Both will be measured by our character—going the extra mile to help someone in need, being faithful in our relationships and responsibilities, doing ordinary things well, and trusting always in an all-good and compassionate God who is ever near and will guide us safely to our heavenly dwelling place.

Twenty-First Sunday
in Ordinary Time

How many play golf? A golf friend told me, "Life is too short … so stop fretting … make the best of each day." He then emphasized his point. "In 1923, Charles Schwab was president of the largest steel company in America; Edward Hopson, president of the largest gas company; and Jesse Livermore, the 'Great Bear' on Wall Street. What became of them? One died flat broke, the second lost his wits, and the third committed suicide."

My friend went on to say that in the same year, the greatest golfer was Gene Sarazen. Winner of both the US Open and the PGA Championship, Sarazen enjoyed golf into his nineties and had a keen intellect until the day he died at age ninety-seven. My friend then concluded, "Stop fretting and start playing golf."

I said, "Okay, I'll take up golf again."

The word of God focuses on a prophet in the eighth century before Jesus (the 700s). Isaiah denounced a royal official who had abused his office. He most likely compromised his integrity. The king replaced him with someone who had integrity, an ethical conscience. The author's words challenge us to always try to do the right thing (Isa 22:19–23).

In his letter to the Christian community at Rome, Paul marveled at the awesome wisdom of God, whose saving grace abounds everywhere. Our God, Paul proclaimed, is a God worthy of our worship. Paul invited us to stand in awe at the wonders of God—for example, the recent solar eclipse—and to thank God for the gift of our lives and our many other blessings, especially family, faith, and friends (Rom 11:33–36).

In the Gospel according to Matthew, Jesus asked, "Who do people say I am?" Peter recognized who Jesus is: the Messiah, the fulfillment of the hopes of ancient Israel, the anointed one, the Christos (Mt 16:13–20). Jesus then made Peter the rock, the leader of his community of disciples, the church. Today it is a global faith community made up of more than 1.2 billion saints and sinners. Jesus gave Peter a special role that became known as the "primacy of Peter." Pope Francis is the 266th successor to Peter.

This global faith community has many heroes and heroines, who teach us about true purpose, the spiritual life, and our relationship with God. Through their lives and writings, these saints can lift us up out of ourselves and into the awesome mystery we call God, to paraphrase Paul's letter.

Today I would like to highlight one of these heroes, Benedict of Nursia, whose life in the sixth century inspired hundreds of thousands to commit themselves to seeking God, especially in a faith community, in common liturgical prayer, and in service to their fellow human beings.

Benedict, well educated in Rome, sought God initially in silence at a hermitage and then established a monastic community at Monte Cassino, now a UNESCO world heritage site, near Naples, Italy.

Benedict crystallized the best of the monastic tradition in his "Rule of Life" for men and women. His initial followers gathered eight times a day for liturgical prayer. They ate meals together, often in silence. The Rule of Benedict can be summed up in a Latin motto, *Ora et labora* (Pray and work).

Benedict's style of monastic life spread so rapidly throughout Europe that the sixth and seventh centuries became known to some as the Benedictine centuries. Amid chaotic times, the abbeys began to take on the functions of education, government, trade, and health care. Some abbeys excelled in evangelization and liturgy. By the ninth and tenth centuries, the Benedictine abbeys were essential pillars of early medieval life, with all its related problems.

With the founding of the abbey at Cluny in France in 910, a reform movement began, which reemphasized the spiritual life for men and women, as found in the Rule of Benedict.

Today a confederation of Benedictine abbeys continues the essential features of the sixth-century rule, seeking God in a common life of prayer and service.

Benedictine spirituality particularly invites us to enter more fully into the liturgical life of the church by participating in the Eucharist, praying the psalms, and reexperiencing the story of our salvation in the liturgical calendar.

First, we enter more deeply into the Eucharist. The Eucharist communicates two realities. First, Jesus gives his body and blood, his life, as a sacrifice of reconciliation between God and us and as proof of God's love for us. Second, Jesus commands us to renew this sacred action by making that sacrifice present through the bread and wine.

Jesus instituted the Eucharist because he wanted to be with us until the end-time—not only through the presence of his Spirit but also through his transformed body.

Bread and wine mystically become the living Christ, transformed from mortality to immortality, corruption to incorruptibility. How can this be? It's a mystery of faith. We believe in the all-powerful and ever-creative word of God.

And what is the purpose of the Eucharist? To form us into one faith community. St. Paul wrote, "Because the loaf of bread is one, we, though many, are one body, for we all partake of the one loaf" (1 Cor 10:17). And this bread we eat and this blood we drink should not only form us into a community of deeper faith but also empower us to reach out compassionately to the people around us. Yes, we go forth from the Eucharist to "wash the feet" of our brothers and sisters, so to speak, in daily life.

Second, Benedictine spirituality invites us to pray the psalms, which were so central to their life of prayer. The psalms are songs and prayers, mostly attributed to King David and gradually formed into a biblical collection of five books in the second century before Jesus. Intended to be sung, these 150 poems express a range of human emotions, from depression to joy. They are hymns of praise to God, community laments in light of a national disaster, royal psalms for a special occasion, and individual laments and thanksgivings.

Third, Benedictine spirituality invites us to reexperience the story of our salvation through the liturgical calendar. This cycle begins with Advent (where we reexperience the hope of our forebears for a Messiah), then moves to Christmas or the actual birth of the Messiah, then through Lent to the dying and rising of Jesus at Easter, and finally, after the Sundays in Ordinary time, to the end of the liturgical year where Jesus Christ comes in glory in the Feast of Christ the King. In this feast, we reach the end of the human story as we know it, when Jesus Christ will hand over the kingdom to God our Father at the end-time.

Yes, St. Benedict, a hero like so many other holy men and women in Christianity, inspires us to seek God in our daily lives, especially through the Eucharist, the psalms, and the liturgical calendar. Why? So that we, reenergized in the life of God, may become the hands and feet and voice and ears of the living Christ in our everyday lives.

Twenty-Second Sunday
in Ordinary Time

The Labor Day weekend, for many people in the United States, signals the end of summer and the start of school.

Which reminds me of a story about a college-bound student, a doctor, a lawyer, and a Franciscan friar in a small private plane. Suddenly the plane's engine conked out. The pilot grabbed a parachute, told the passengers he had a family of six to support and bailed out. Unfortunately, there were only three parachutes left. The doctor grabbed one, saying, "The medical profession needs my specialty skills," and he jumped out. The lawyer said, "I'm one of the smartest litigators in the country, so I'm taking this parachute," and he jumped out. The friar said to the student, "You're a student and have dreams to fulfill. Take the last parachute." The student replied, "You take it. I'll use this one. The smartest lawyer just jumped with my backpack."

Moral of the story: we may not be as smart as we think.

Seriously, Labor Day is an invitation to take pride in our work. Whatever our life's work is, may we do it well.

Isn't that what holiness is all about—doing our life's work as best we can? You've heard the biblical wisdom that says God sends each person into this life with a special message to deliver, a special song to sing, a special act of love to bestow. Yes, each of us has a purpose in life.

The word of God today takes us back to the seventh century before Jesus (the 600s). Jeremiah wasn't happy. "God tricked me," Jeremiah said, prophesying doom and gloom about Jerusalem (Jer 20:7–9). You've heard the saying—"If you don't like the message, don't ..."

Shoot the messenger. That's precisely what the Hebrews did. They beat up Jeremiah badly. From now on, Jeremiah said, he would keep his mouth shut. But he couldn't. The word of God is like a fire that consumed Jeremiah, burning him up if he didn't shout out God's word.

We might ask ourselves whether we speak up when we see wrongs done. If not, when will we? And if we don't, who will?

St. Paul, in his letter to the Christian community at Rome, urged us to dedicate our lives—our talents and energies—to God (Rom 12:1–2). In light of Paul's letter, we might ask whether our everyday attitudes and behaviors are pleasing to God.

In the Gospel according to Matthew, Jesus predicted his passion, death, and resurrection. The impetuous Peter shouted, "God forbid. No such thing will happen to you, Lord" (Mt 16:21–27). But God's ways are not ours. Through the cross, the central symbol of Christianity will emerge: the resurrection, new life. Our faith proclaims that hidden within the mystery of Jesus's death is the glory of his resurrection. And so too hidden in our own dying is resurrection, life eternal.

I have been reflecting on the guidance of some of the great saints these last two weeks, Augustine and Benedict, among holy men and women whose lives and writings can lift us up out of our routine and take us into the awesome presence of God.

Today I would like to highlight a stellar thirteenth-century thinker whose work as a spiritual guide is still relevant in the twenty-first century. Thomas Aquinas can mentor us about our true purpose, the spiritual life, and our relationship with God.

Born in 1226, Thomas began his education at the Benedictine abbey at Monte Cassino in Italy and continued his studies at the University of Naples, where he was fascinated with the writings of Aristotle and other philosophers. There he met the Dominican friars, joined them, and began forming his life on the four pillars of Dominican spirituality. Those are common prayer, especially the Eucharist and Liturgy of the Hours; a community life; the study of the mysteries of our faith; and gospel preaching. In fact, a popular Dominican Latin motto is *laudare, benedicere, praedicare* (to praise, to bless, to preach [God]).

Thomas completed his theological studies at the University of Paris, became a renowned professor and preacher, and eventually began constructing a "Summa Theologiae," a comprehensive study of our Christian faith. Ideas included, Where do we come from (God)? Where are we going (to God)? How do we get there (practicing virtues and avoiding vices)? And who and what give us the capacity to go there (Jesus Christ through the sacraments)? Faith, Thomas argued, is a gift from God; it's also a risk but a reasonable one. Faith and reason, Thomas contended, are compatible.

Thomas's monumental summary examines 512 questions, many of which we ourselves might ask. His process is rigorous. A question is stated (for example, whether there's a God); then there are arguments against and for the author's own point of view, and a reply to arguments with which the author disagrees. Colleges and universities today would be well served with a process like Thomas's in debates about important issues in light of the pervasiveness of political correctness on a number of campuses.

Sacraments, especially for Thomas, are tangible encounters with the living Christ. By tangible, we mean it involves our senses. And by encounter, it's a meeting in which the living Christ communicates with us personally, as he did with people in Judea and Galilee centuries before. The seven sacraments, special moments when the living Christ acts through us, the community of his disciples, may be grouped as follows:

- Sacraments of initiation (baptism, confirmation, Eucharist)
- Sacraments of healing (reconciliation, anointing of the sick)
- Sacraments of commitment (marriage and holy orders)

Near the end of his life, Thomas had a vision of God so powerful that he stopped writing, even as his assistants urged him to complete the "Summa." He humbly replied to their request, "After what I have seen, all that I have written seems to me like so much straw." His voluminous writings seemed so worthless to him in light of his mystical experience of God.

Thomas died in 1274, but his work endures. It's worthwhile reading. A theologian par excellence, his writings demonstrate that there are reasonable arguments for faith in God. For example, the design of the universe presupposes a designer; order presupposes an orderer. Thomas was also a mystic who experienced God in prayer and a poet whose classic hymns are still sung today—for example, "O Salutaris Hostia" and "Tantum ergo Sacramentum."

Yes, St. Thomas Aquinas, a master in the spiritual life, invites us to discipline our lives so we can nurture our faith in God. Take time every day to tune into the presence of God. Explore participation in parish faith circles. Gather on weekends to celebrate the presence of the living Christ in the liturgy of word and sacrament. Study the Bible—for example, in our parish study groups. Understand church teachings better by visiting recommended Catholic websites.

I conclude by asking God to make this prayer of St. Thomas Aquinas our own:

> Grant me, O Lord my God,
> a mind to know you, a heart to seek you,
> wisdom to find you, conduct pleasing to you,
> faithful perseverance in waiting for you, and
> a hope of finally embracing you. Amen.

TWENTY-THIRD SUNDAY
IN ORDINARY TIME

Y ou may have heard about the Jesuit who crashed into another car. The other driver was a Franciscan friar. The Franciscan insisted, "It was your fault." The Jesuit replied, "You look shaken up. You could probably use a shot of whiskey." He handed him a flask. The Franciscan drank and said, "Thank you." The Jesuit said, "You still look rattled. Have another." He did. "One more," said the Jesuit, "and you'll feel fine." After a third drink, the Franciscan said, "Why don't you have a drink?" The Jesuit replied, "I'll wait until after the police arrive."

Watch out for those Jesuits. Seriously, I'll say more about the Jesuits later.

The word of God takes us back to the sixth century before Jesus (the 500s). God called Ezekiel to be a "watchman," answerable to God for the spiritual well-being of the Hebrews. Ezekiel's mission was to challenge the Hebrews to do the right thing, to live up to the demands of God's covenant (Eze 33:7–9).

The author may be urging us to be watchmen as well; we should be speaking up when we see wrongs done and living up to the demands of discipleship with Jesus. How relevant are the words of the eighteenth-century British statesman Edmund Burke. "The only thing necessary for evil to triumph is for good people to do nothing."

In his letter to the Christian community in Rome, Paul said, "You shall love your neighbor as yourself" (Rom 13:8–10). Yes, we love God to the extent that we care for one another. And who is my neighbor? The person next to me—at home, in the workplace, in the shopping mall, and in the parish community. If we want to know who our neighbor is, we should simply look around us. Paul's words may ask us, Do we offer a helping hand to others?

In the Gospel according to Matthew, Jesus asked us to settle our differences—not by complaining to everyone else about people whose behavior annoys us but by going directly to them first to resolve our conflicts. Conflicts are inevitable in human relationships, but if we deal with them constructively, they can create even better friendships (Mt 18:15–20).

I can imagine Jesus saying to us, "Always focus on the behavior, not the personality; avoid negative name-calling. Identify the problem. Manage your emotions, stay positive, and offer solutions. And be trustworthy, open, fair, and calm." St. Paul wrote centuries ago, "Love does not brood over injuries." All of us must be willing to forgive and work together to create positive relationships.

I have been reflecting these last few weeks on the guidance of some of the great movers and shakers in Christianity. They are Augustine, Benedict, Thomas Aquinas—among holy men and women whose lives and writings can lift us up out of our routine and into a deeper relationship with God.

Today I would like to highlight Ignatius of Loyola, the sixteenth-century founder of the Society of Jesus, the Jesuits. Ignatius's masterpiece, the *Spiritual Exercises*, can give guidance about our true purpose, our spiritual life, and our relationship with God.

Ignatius, born in the Basque region of Spain, lived in the sixteenth century, a revolutionary era that split Christianity in Europe into Protestants and Catholics. Ignatius first became a page boy in Castile's royal court, then a military officer. Gravely injured in battle, he had a long convalescence and started to change his way of life. On a pilgrimage to the Holy Land, he stopped at the Benedictine abbey of Montserrat, near Barcelona, then stayed at Manresa, where he began outlining the *Spiritual Exercises*, his own search for God in all things.

On his return from the Holy Land, Ignatius pursued his education. In Paris, he and six other men pledged to live a way of life in the company of Jesus. Pope Paul III gave his approval to the Society of Jesus in 1540. Members vowed to live in the midst of the world with their eyes focused on God, with Jesus as their companion, and with a mission to dedicate themselves *Ad Maiorem Dei Gloriam* (to the greater glory of God).

Ignatius was elected superior general and guided the society as it grew quickly.

The newly discovered lands of the sixteenth century beckoned the Jesuits as missionary disciples. They set sail for the Far East, the Americas, and Africa to speak to the minds and hearts of indigenous people about the things of God (the gospel). They did this all for the greater glory of God. Today the Jesuits number more than sixteen thousand in over 110 countries, with twenty-eight Jesuit-sponsored colleges and universities in the United States alone.

Ignatius recognized the priority of the spiritual life. He gave us missionary disciples formed in the *Spiritual Exercises* as a guide to their life with God and also myriad ministries where Jesuits serve God's people however and wherever the church calls. Education—religious education, in particular—was a priority for Ignatius in the Reformation era.

Jesuit spirituality emphasizes discernment. Learning to discern where the Spirit is prompting and guiding us is a lifelong task for all of us. Discernment, of course, is not only learning to sense the presence of God within our own selves but also analyzing social situations in light of gospel values. Discernment includes reading the signs of the times and responding to poverty, injustice, and violence in our world by doing our best to right wrongs.

Jesuit spirituality invites us to deepen our own lives with God through the *Spiritual Exercises* so we can become missionary disciples to others, bearers of the good news that Jesus Christ is risen, alive, and among us, transforming this universe into a new earth.

The exercises themselves are an organized process of spiritual growth with a variety of tools. These include rules for discernment of the spirit and for "thinking with the church," an examination of conscience, meditations, and various prayer forms. Their purpose is to free us from earthly worries, to find God "in all things," and to recommit ourselves to Jesus and service.

A seasoned guide is indispensable in this process. The meditations in the first stage aim to free us from self-centered attitudes and behaviors that get in the way of following Jesus. The second stage meditates on the life of Jesus—for example, his Sermon on the Mount, his ministry of healing and teaching so we can model ourselves after Jesus. The third stage focuses on the Last Supper, the passion and death of Jesus, and signs of his tremendous love for us. The fourth stage concentrates on the risen Jesus so we can become his hands and feet, and voice and eyes in the world, finding God in all things.

Yes, embracing Jesus and finding God in all things were the passions of Ignatius of Loyola. I close with a prayer of Ignatius that could well be our own.

> Take, O Lord, and receive all
> my liberty, my memory, my understanding, and my entire will,
> all that I have and possess.
> You have given all to me; to you, O Lord, I return it.
> All is yours; dispose of it wholly according to your will.
> Give me your love and your grace; for this is enough for me.
> Amen.

Twenty-Fourth Sunday
in Ordinary Time

Hurricane Irma hit several areas of Florida and the Caribbean very hard; let's keep the people affected by Irma in our thoughts and prayers, and lend a helping hand in next weekend's special collection if we can. We in St. Petersburg prepared for the worst but were blessed with downgraded category-one high winds, though many were still affected by power outages and downed trees.

During the hurricane, I thought of the biblical story of Noah and the ark, and I pondered few lessons from that story:

1. Plan ahead. When Noah built the ark, it wasn't raining.
2. Stay fit. We may have to do something big.
3. Don't miss the boat.
4. Speed isn't always an advantage. On the ark, snails were with cheetahs.
5. The ark was built by amateurs; the *Titanic* was made by professionals.
6. No matter how severe the storm, with God there's a rainbow waiting.

Yes, there are a few lessons to consider in the aftermath of the storm.

The word of God takes us back to the second century before Jesus. The wisdom of Sirach is one of Israel's many spiritual guides, a collection of advice about how to live well. It emphasizes the golden rule—"Do unto others as you would have them do unto you." Practice virtue: faith in God, honesty, compassion, discipline, and responsibility. Here the author challenges us to seek forgiveness in our broken relationships with God and with one another. God forgives us to the extent that we forgive (Sir 27:30–28:7).

In his letter to the Christian community at Rome, Paul acknowledged God's complete sovereignty over life and death. He urged us to live not for ourselves but for others. Imitate God and live a godlike life. Paul emphasized that we belong to Jesus Christ. Christ lives. And because he lives, we live forever (Rom 14:7–9).

In the Gospel according to Matthew, Peter asked Jesus whether he had to forgive a person who had wronged him "as many as seven times." In other words, when do we start getting even? Jesus responded with an even more outrageous number, "seventy-seven times." Jesus then made his point with a parable. Worker number one owes a huge amount of money (say the equivalent of $1 million). The king cancels his debt. Then worker number one runs into worker number two, who owes him a small amount (say $100). What does worker number one do? He grabs worker number two by the throat, chokes him, and says, "Pay me now, or I'll put you in jail." When the king hears this, he summons worker number one and says, "I canceled your debt. Shouldn't you have done the same?" And the king throws worker number one into jail (Mt 18:21–35).

The lesson is simple: God forgives so much, so why can't we forgive so little? Forgiveness doesn't necessarily mean we forget. Nor does it mean we have to relate to or like the one who's wronged us.

Forgiveness in the final analysis is a decision to will the good of the other, even though we may continue harboring negative feelings about the person. It's a decision to let go of wrongs done to us and move on with our lives.

I have been reflecting these last few weeks on the guidance of some of the great names in Christianity, holy men and women whose lives and writings can lift us into a more intimate friendship with God. Today I would like to highlight two Carmelite icons. The Carmelites go back to the early thirteenth century, to a community on Mount Carmel in Israel. The 1247 "Rule of St. Albert" defines their spirituality as

Christ-centered, Eucharistic, and biblical, "thinking with the church," devoted to the Virgin Mary, inspired by the prophet Elijah, and living together in community. This Carmelite movement spread rapidly into Europe, attracting men (friars), women (nuns), and laypeople.

In sixteenth-century Spain, at a time of dramatic exploration and religious upheaval, Teresa of Avila entered the Carmelite monastery in Avila, a UNESCO world heritage site. Teresa, along with fellow Carmelite John of the Cross, became an energetic reformer, despite intense resistance. They traveled to Carmelite monasteries and established numerous discalced—"barefoot"—communities emphasizing the contemplative aspect of their rule.

Teresa's writings had great influence in spiritual circles. *Interior Castle* is her masterpiece, written when she was sixty-two years old. She illustrated the individual's ascent to God in the imagery of a castle, where the triune God dwells in seven mansions or chambers. These are comparable to the classic stages of prayer: the purgative way (trying to please God), the illuminative way (being pleasing to God), and the unitive way (ecstatic experience of God). With grace, Teresa described persevering for twenty years before she had a mystical experience. Bernini's sculpture, *St. Teresa in Ecstasy*, captures splendidly this doctor of the church.

I love this prayerful reflection of Teresa of Avila. "Let nothing upset you, Let nothing startle you, all things pass; God does not change. Patience wins all it seeks. Whoever has God lacks nothing; God alone is enough." Teresa is a model of our own search for God; she experienced God daily in prayer and work.

Therese of Lisieux, another Carmelite icon, lived and died in the late nineteenth century in the obscurity of a cloister in Normandy, France. We know about her through the remarkable autobiography she was asked to write, *The Story of a Soul*. At fifteen, Therese joined two of her sisters at the Carmelite monastery and pursued a spiritual path she came to call the "little way." She died at twenty-four, still struggling with doubts and yet holding a crucifix tenderly as she spoke her dying words—"My God, I love You."

So, what is Therese's "little way" that anyone can follow? For me, it includes three ingredients. Yes, good things come in threes (Father, Son, and Spirit).

First, Therese realized her own insignificance. Think about it. More than seven billion people live on this planet—perhaps billions before, perhaps billions after. There are maybe ten trillion planets in our galaxy alone and at least two hundred billion galaxies. Wow! Yet God gave us significance. God, who is love, created us in love so God could be one with us. Therese personified humility, gratitude to God that she even existed.

Second, Therese recognized that God loved her unconditionally. That's why she had a childlike trust and lived completely dependent on the love of her Father in heaven, and she was always receptive to whatever gifts God bestowed on her.

Finally, because God loved her unconditionally, Therese loved God unconditionally, even though she often wondered where God was. She did small things extraordinarily well out of love for God. She accepted the will of God in the daily routine of cloistered life. In every situation, Therese willed the good of the other, no matter how annoying they were.

Therese's "little way" can be a spiritual guide for us. It can include having gratitude to God, trusting in God, and doing ordinary things well out of love for God.

These two Carmelite icons, Teresa of Avila and Therese of Lisieux, challenge us to integrate prayer into our daily lives and walk into the awesome light of God forever.

TWENTY-FIFTH SUNDAY
IN ORDINARY TIME

I just read about a ninety-plus grandfather who was almost stone deaf. Without telling anyone in the family, he decided to buy a high-tech set of hearing aids; they worked perfectly. When the grandfather went back to the audiologist for his check-up, the audiologist said to him, "I'll bet your family was really surprised and delighted to discover you could hear so well again." The grandfather replied, "I haven't told my family yet. I just sit around and listen to what they're saying about me. I've already changed my will three times." Moral of the story: be careful what you say.

The word of God from Isaiah takes us to the sixth century before Jesus. The Hebrews would be freed from Babylonia so they could begin rebuilding Jerusalem. The author challenged the Hebrews to seek God in their everyday lives, to call on God. And then the author spoke of the complete otherness of God. God's ways and thoughts are not ours (Isa 55:6–9). The author may prompt us to ask, "When we hear the word *God*, what do we think of?" The Bible gives us many splendid images—a walking companion in Genesis, a God who shares his wisdom, a God as tender as a mother in the book of Isaiah: "Can a mother forget her infant? And even if she should, I will never forget you." In the New Testament, the image of God in the parables of the good shepherd and the prodigal son are balanced with the image in the parable of the last judgment. Yes, there are many splendid biblical images—yet all fail to fully capture the inexhaustible reality of God who loves us unconditionally.

In his letter to the Christian community at Philippi in Greece, Paul spoke about his fondness for this community. Here he wrote from prison in Turkey. Paul's life hung in the balance. He didn't know whether he would be executed or freed. He was torn between wanting to die so he could be with Christ and wanting to live so he could continue ministering to the communities he'd founded. In the end, Paul was confident that he would be set free, and he urged the Philippians to live a life worthy of their calling. Paul's words challenge us to do the same (Phil 1:20–24, 27).

In the Gospel according to Matthew, Jesus spoke about workers in a vineyard. Some were hired at the beginning of the day, while others were hired at the end. Yet all received the same day's wage. We might complain that this story isn't fair. Shouldn't those who worked twelve hours be paid more than those who worked only one hour? From a human point of view, the situation isn't fair. But the parable isn't about fairness. It's about generosity, God's generosity to us. Jesus challenged us to be generous, especially with our time and talent—and yes, our treasure if we can (Mt 20:1–16).

Over these last few weeks, I've been reflecting on the spirituality of holy men and women whose lives and writings can help nourish us spiritually and lift us out of our routine into a deeper life with God. Today I highlight Blessed John Henry Newman, the influential nineteenth-century priest, popular preacher, writer, and theologian whose writings introduced the spirit of the Second Vatican Council a century later.

Newman spent the first half of his life as an Anglican (a.k.a. Episcopalian) and the second as a Catholic. Born in London, he entered Oxford University at age fifteen and eventually served as vicar of the university church for seventeen years. He published eight volumes of sermons, a classic in Christian spirituality.

The high point of Newman's Anglican career was his influential role in the Oxford movement, an intellectual effort to return to the sources of our faith—the Bible, the sacraments, belief statements, authority in the church, and the apostolic succession of bishops.

Newman's research eventually convinced him that Rome was

the home of the true church. In 1845, Newman was received into the Catholic Church. Two years later he was ordained a Catholic priest. Returning to England, Newman founded oratory houses in Birmingham and London, and then he served as rector of the Catholic University of Ireland, which inspired his landmark book, *The Idea of a University*.

Newman wrote forty books and twenty-one thousand surviving letters. Most famous are his *Apologia Pro Vita Sua* (*A Defense of His Life*), his spiritual autobiography, and his classic *Essay on the Development of Christian Doctrine*, which describes the continuity between what was revealed and believed in first-century Christianity and what is believed now.

The fullness of revelation, Newman emphasized, resides in the person of Jesus Christ. Belief statements try to capture, but never do so fully, the inexhaustible reality of the God-man. Hence, Christianity must develop just as we grow. We change, yet we're the same people. So too with Christianity. And there must be an authority on the truth or falsity of these developments.

Newman also was a supporter of Christian unity at a time when Christianity was divided and religious bigotry commonplace.

In particular, he was a pioneer in emphasizing the active role of the laity in the church. He wrote that the "Spirit dwells in the Church and in the hearts of the faithful as in a temple."

Newman's writings reflect the spirit of the Second Vatican Council (1962–1965). The church is always reformable, holy yet made of sinners. Revelation is a person, Jesus Christ. In other words, God reveals himself to us in Jesus, and we describe this revelation in belief statements (for example, the Nicene Creed). Word and sacrament mutually reinforce one another. The Eucharist is "the summit toward which the activity of the Church is directed" and "the font from which all her power flows."

In special recognition for Newman's dedicated work, Pope Leo XIII made him a Cardinal Deacon in 1879.

Newman died in 1890. His epitaph read, "*Ex umbris et imaginibus in veritatem*" (Out of shadows and images into truth).

In relation to today's word of God, I highlight two awesome prayers by Newman, the first about purpose in life:

God has created me to do Him some definite service. He has

committed some work to me which He has not committed to another. I have my mission. I may never know it in this life, but ... I shall do His work ... Therefore, I will trust Him, whatever, wherever I am. I can never be thrown away. If I am in sickness, my sickness may serve Him, in perplexity, my perplexity may serve Him ... God knows what He is about. He may take away my friends. He may throw me among strangers. He may make me feel desolate, make my spirits sink, hide my future from me. Still, He knows what He is about.

The second prayer holds one of my favorite images of God: light. Newman's poem "The Pillar of the Cloud," written while he recovered from severe illness, was made into a hymn. Here is a very recognizable verse of Newman's poem:

> Lead, Kindly Light, amid the encircling gloom, Lead Thou me on!
> The night is dark, and I am far from home, Lead Thou me on!
> Keep Thou my feet; I do not ask to see the distant scene; one step enough for me ...
> So long Your power hath blest me, sure it still will lead me on ... into God's eternal light.

May we all find purpose in life, and may the light of Jesus Christ lead us on into our heavenly dwelling place. Amen.

TWENTY-SIXTH SUNDAY
IN ORDINARY TIME

On Wednesday, October 4, we Franciscans celebrate the Feast of St. Francis of Assisi.

Years ago, at a festive liturgy in New York City, the archbishop was the principal celebrant. He'd had a very grueling day. But he still had our extravaganza liturgy at 5 o'clock in the evening. The choir sang all the hymn verses, the Gloria, the Credo and so forth. The homilist spoke for forty-five minutes. And the pastor introduced to the archbishop everyone in the long offertory procession, with a commentary about each.

After communion, the exhausted archbishop was about to conclude the endless liturgy, when lo and behold music began, and a woman in a flowing gown did an elaborate liturgical dance, which to the archbishop resembled Salome in the Bible dancing for King Herod. The now-irritable archbishop leaned over to the pastor and deadpanned, "If she wants your head on a platter, she's got it." Moral of the story: timing is everything.

The word of God carries us back in our imaginations to the sixth century before Jesus to the prophet Ezekiel. The Hebrews were blaming God and everybody else but themselves for their misfortunes—the occupation of their land by a foreign power, the destruction of Jerusalem, their deportation to Babylonia. They were ready to put God on trial. C. S. Lewis wrote about this tendency in his book *God in the Dock*. The Hebrews forgot that maturity begins where blame ends. We must take responsibility for our lives. Ezekiel here described God bestowing life on a repentant individual, a person living a God-centered life (Eze 18:25–28). Ezekiel's words may be asking us, What kind of life are we living? A God-centered or self-centered life?

Paul challenged the Christian community at Philippi in Greece to assume the mind-set of Jesus, to be at peace with one another, and to serve one another humbly. He then quoted a stirring early Christian hymn about Jesus who, though one in glory with God, emptied himself, becoming one of us. He even died crucified like a common criminal. And because of this, God greatly exalted him. This ancient hymn celebrates two central truths of our faith: the mystery of the incarnation and the birth of the God-man and the mystery of the resurrection. In the tragedy of Good Friday, there was the triumph of Easter (Phil 2:1–11).

In the Gospel according to Matthew, Jesus told a parable or story about two sons. One is smooth talking but doesn't do what he's asked; the other is perhaps argumentative but eventually does what he's asked. Jesus made his point: sinners initially said no to God but then had a "change of heart" and pursued a godlike life. But you, the religious leaders, Jesus said, say yes to God but continue unrepentant in self-centered attitudes and behaviors (Mt 21:28–32).

Jesus concluded that God forgives us unconditionally if we repent, if we have a change of heart and pursue a godlike life.

These last few weeks, I've been reflecting on the spirituality of holy men and women whose lives and writings can lift us out of our routine and push us into a deeper life with God. I conclude this little series with Francis of Assisi, whose feast day we celebrate Wednesday.

Who was Francis? This patron saint of animals and the environment has been portrayed as a hippie flower child, a peacemaker, a mystic, a reformer, and a poet. But who really was this thirteenth-century founder of the movement known as the Franciscans?

Francis came from a middle-class Italian family. He went off to the wars in that region and failed miserably. Then one night he had a dream, which compelled him to return to Assisi. He began to wrestle with the fundamental questions of life: What am I living for? What is the purpose of my life?

In silence and prayer, Francis began his own search for God. Eventually he gave up everything he had; and in that experience of nothingness, he found everything—God—an all-good God who became flesh in Jesus of Nazareth and is alive by the power of the Spirit.

Francis began to pursue the gospel way of life in a literal fashion. In time, men and women began to gather and form what we know as the worldwide Franciscan movement. Clare, a holy woman of Assisi, became a close friend and confidante of Francis, and she with her companions consecrated themselves to God as "poor ladies" or "Poor Clares" in prayer and service while living a cloistered life.

Does the thirteenth-century Francis have anything to say to us in the twenty-first century? Of course! We can summarize his message in three incidents.

First, in 1206, as Francis prayed before the crucifix in the tumbledown chapel of San Damiano, outside the city walls of Assisi, he heard Jesus on the crucifix whisper, "Francis, rebuild my house, which you see is falling into ruins." Francis began to renovate the building and eventually renewed the church in the high middle ages. Francis at San Damiano challenges us to build up the relationships in our household, workplace, parish, and community. How? Begin by being faithful in our commitments to one another and courageous in trying to do the right thing. Above all, by praying that God will sustain us in our daily lives.

Another incident that captures the message of Francis was his encounter with a leper. As Francis rode on horseback one day, he saw a man with leprosy. Francis started to ride away. But no! He slowly dismounted and embraced the leper. He saw in that person the broken image of God. We instinctively may want to get away from some people just as Francis was tempted, to ride away, so to speak. Francis's embrace of the leper challenges us to help the needy, to practice the corporal and spiritual works of mercy. There are so many ways in which we can become healers, peacemakers, and comforters. All we must do is "just do it."

A final incident took place at La Verna, not far from Florence, Italy, in 1224. Francis was praying to God, and suddenly he experienced the marks of the crucified Jesus in his hands, feet, and side. This incident captures the depth of Francis's prayer life. It was such a close friendship that God gifted him with the stigmata. Francis's example challenges us to intensify our own lives with God, especially in prayer.

May Francis of Assisi—who made the person of Jesus Christ his way, his truth, and his life; who realized his own absolute poverty and thus his utter dependency upon God; who found the image of God everywhere and in all creatures; who embraced the brotherhood of man and the Fatherhood of God; and who cared especially for the needy—inspire us to deepen our life with God, build up the relationships in our families and communities, and reach out with helping hands as near and far as we are able.

I pray that this prayer of St. Francis may be ours as well.

> Most High, glorious God,
> enlighten the darkness of my heart
> and give me
> true faith, certain hope, and perfect love …
> that I may carry out
> Your holy will. Amen.

Twenty-Seventh Sunday
in Ordinary Time

I often look at perseverance as an element of virtues. Take Columbus Day. Christopher Columbus for me symbolizes perseverance. A sailor and explorer, he calculated that if the world was round, he could reach the east by sailing west. No one he knew would finance a voyage. But eventually some advisers convinced Ferdinand and Isabella of Spain. The rest is history. Columbus was a skilled navigator of vision and perseverance. He never gave up on his dream, and neither should we give up on ours. Not all will come true, but some will if we persevere.

I read about a pastor who had to renovate his parish church. Unbelievably a contractor said he would do the renovation at no charge but on one condition. The pastor should never interfere until the renovations were done. How could the pastor refuse? When the job was complete, the contractor invited the pastor in. He was astounded to see only one pew. But wait! Once people filled it, up came another pew electronically from the floor, and another. The congregation filled the pews as needed. No empty pews!

Then the pastor went to the pulpit and began practicing his homily, and a few minutes later, he disappeared beneath the floor. He emerged from the basement and asked what happened. The contractor said, "I installed a high-tech feature in the pulpit: a trap door opens after eight minutes. After all, enough is enough."

The word of God carries us back in our imaginations to the eighth century before Jesus (the 700s BC). Isaiah told an allegory or story about a vineyard. It's a lover's lament. The owner is God; the vineyard is the Jewish people, the bearers of God's revelation; and the wild or bad grapes are their infidelities. God was deeply disappointed with them for their infidelities (Isa 5:1–7).

Isaiah may be asking us, How faithful are we to our commitments? How courageous are we in trying to do the right thing?

In his letter to the Christian community at Philippi in Greece, Paul challenged us not to be anxious about our lives but to make our needs known to God in prayer. Paul then urged us to focus on what is honorable, true, and good. Good advice! (Phil 4:6–9).

In the Gospel according to Matthew, Jesus told a parable similar to Isaiah's. God is still the owner of the vineyard; the Jewish people are the vineyard; and the tenants are their religious leaders. The message is simple enough: those who try to do the right thing, who live a God-centered life, will inherit the kingdom of God (Mt 21:33–43).

Today I would like to take up Paul's challenge: "Have no anxiety at all." Many of us carry the burden of worry throughout our lives; most of these worries never materialize. We forget that Jesus said, "Come to me, all you who are ... burdened, and I will give you rest." In other words, keep company with Jesus, and we'll be at peace with ourselves.

A book titled *Affluenza* points out that almost a quarter of Britain suffers serious emotional distress, such as depression and anxiety, and another quarter are on the verge thereof. Put bluntly, half of Britain is in a bad way. Are we Americans also in a bad way?

Jesus invites us to commit to him the burden of our fears, worries, and anxieties. Doing so will make all the difference. Jesus bears our burdens because he cares for us.

We carry other types of burdens as well. Failure can be a burden. The apostle Peter denied knowing Jesus. Peter realized, as most of us do from time to time, that he had failed Jesus. A sense of failure can be a great burden. But later, Jesus met with Peter and reinstated him. With Jesus, failure is never final. Though Peter failed him, Jesus took the burden, forgave him, reinstated him, and used him as powerfully as anyone in history.

An injustice done to us can be a burden. One of the many things

Jesus had to bear was a rigged trial. A basic principle of a fair system of justice is that it's up to the prosecution to prove the case—innocent until proven guilty beyond a reasonable doubt.

Pontius Pilate concluded, "I find no basis for a charge against him." But the crowd shouted, "No, not him! Give us Barabbas!" Jesus, the innocent, was condemned. Barabbas, the sinful, went free. The symbolism is clear. Jesus, the innocent, died so we, the sinful, could be set free from death and have a relationship with God forever. Again, Jesus bore the burden of our sin.

Guilt can be a burden. God has given us a moral sense, a conscience. Often we feel guilty because we have done something we know is wrong. However, our conscience isn't perfect because we are fallen creatures. Sometimes we experience false guilt. We feel guilty about things that aren't actually our fault. At other times we don't feel guilty about things we should feel guilty about; in that case we need the Spirit of God to awaken our consciences.

Yes, Jesus takes on our burdens—fears, worries and anxieties, injustices done to us, and guilt—and gives us rest. In Jesus, we find not only rest but also purpose in life.

Some people seem to have no purpose or goal in life. Others have goals but the wrong ones, and they end up chasing something meaningless. Many climb the ladder of "success" only to find that it's leaning against the wrong wall.

You've heard the saying—"You make a living by what you get but you make a life by what you give." We might begin by trying to be instruments of peace wherever we find division.

It has been said that the greatest days of our lives are the day we were born and the day we find out why. God created us with a purpose (2 Cor 5:5).

The purpose or goal of our lives is to pursue a right relationship with God and a right relationship with others. Paul's main aim was, "We aspire to please God ... For we must all appear before the judgment seat of Christ" (2 Cor 5:9).

But how do we please God in everything? The prophet Micah centuries ago gave us some good, simple advice. He reminded us that our God is a God of unconditional love and unconditional forgiveness.

And what is our response to God's amazing love? The prophet Micah wrote, "Only to do the right and to love goodness, and to walk humbly with our God" (Mic 6:8). This threefold challenge gives us the purpose and goal of our lives: doing the right thing, loving goodness, showing that goodness to as many people as possible, and walking in relationship with God. These three go together.

I close with an African proverb. "If you think you're too small to make a difference, you haven't spent the night with a mosquito." The mosquito makes a difference in an annoying way, but the principle is universal. One person can stop an injustice. One person can be a voice for truth. One person's kindness can save a life. Each life matters.

Twenty-Eighth Sunday

In Ordinary Time

You may have heard the story about a pastor feuding with his choir director. The pastor one Sunday preached about service. Immediately afterward, the choir director played the hymn "I Shall Not Be Moved." The pastor preached on giving. The choir director sang "Jesus Paid It All."

The pastor finally told the congregation that unless something changed, he would consider resigning. The choir director led the hymn "Why Not Tonight?" The pastor finally did resign, explaining that Jesus had led him here but now was leading him to another church. The choir director sang "What a Friend We Have in Jesus." Don't mess with the choir director.

The word of God takes us up to a mountaintop. The author of Isaiah wrote poetically about a future in which God, a victorious warrior, gathers all people together for a banquet. It's a vision of salvation, with no more death or grief. It almost sounds like a party with God, and everyone loves a party (Isa 25:6–10).

Isaiah may be asking us, What is our vision of the future? If it's living in God's presence forever, what are we doing now to make that vision a reality?

In his letter to the Christian community at Philippi in Greece, Paul described his life. Sometimes he had plenty; at other times he didn't have enough. But so be it. What mattered most for Paul was preaching the good news that Jesus is alive. And because he lives, we live. Paul wrote that he could do all things through the God who lived within him. He relied completely on God, who loved him unconditionally (Phil 4:12–14, 19–20).

Paul may be asking us, Do we trust in God's unconditional love for us, especially when things aren't going our way, when what is happening is the opposite of what we want?

In the Gospel according to Matthew, Jesus told a parable or allegory about a king who invites his so-called friends to a banquet. But the king's friends refuse for one reason or another. So the king says, "Forget these fair-weather friends," and goes out into the streets and invites whomever he can find, good as well as bad. But still, the invitation requires appropriate dress. Yes, God invites all people to the banquet of eternal life, but they must be "clothed" in a right relationship with God (Mt 22:1–14).

It's amazing how a banquet or dinner can bring people together. Think of the wonderful things that often take place at our own tables. Families celebrate important transitions—birthdays, graduations, and so forth—around a table.

How many saw the movie *Babette's Feast*? It was a 1987 Academy Award winner. It's also a favorite film of Pope Francis.

Babette, a French chef, finds herself in a small town where its strict and puritanical religiosity makes people hard, cold, and judgmental; they are afraid to enjoy anything or anyone. Babette unexpectedly wins a lottery and spends all her winnings on a huge, delectable feast for the townspeople. As they begin to taste and enjoy the meal, they start to communicate good-naturedly. They even dance! The meal transforms them into warm-hearted human beings.

Babette models self-giving and elicits joy in people, a foretaste of heaven. The toast at the end captures why, I think, Pope Francis likes the movie. Here's a paraphrase of the toast:

> There comes a time when your eyes are opened.
> And we come to realize … that mercy is infinite.
> We need only await it with confidence … and receive
> it with gratitude.

As I reflected on *Babette's Feast*, I thought about our own relationships, especially family ones. Happy families have a good, solid sense of togetherness. They care about one another. They keep in touch; they're hospitable and concerned about elderly relatives. They celebrate birthdays, anniversaries, and other special family milestones such as graduations, baptisms, confirmations, and marriages. They take responsibility for family chores. They spend time together. They set times to eat meals together, and there they share good news as well as bad. They keep their word and thereby build up trust in their relationships. More importantly, they know how to agree to disagree. They try to avoid negative name-calling; they can distinguish the behavior they find objectionable from judgments about that behavior. For example, someone is late. A negative judgment would be, "You're so selfish." The actual behavior is, "You're late." The reasons may be many—for example, an accident on the highway or a last-minute request from the boss. Good relationships avoid blurting out negative name-calling that subtly undermines a relationship. In the end, we may simply agree to disagree. That's okay.

In his letter to the Ephesians, St. Paul asked us to be imitators of God, to live lives of love, just as Christ loved us and gave himself up for us (Eph 5:1–2). What does this life of love look like? In chapters 4 and 5 especially, Paul gave us at least five ingredients for good relationships:

- Be authentic, speak the truth to one another, and try to live a life of honesty and integrity (Eph 4:25). Authenticity makes it easy to admit we're far from perfect. We have our own foibles and peccadilloes. Authenticity also steers us away from hypocrisy.
- Be passionate about what's right. Rev. Martin Luther King Jr., for example, had a passionate hatred against discrimination that led him to champion civil rights. Nelson Mandela had a hatred against apartheid, which led him to champion freedom. Jesus had a righteous anger about the money changers in the temple; this anger led him to throw them out. Anger should result in righting wrongs.
- Paul encouraged the Ephesians to get an honest job so they could help others. Work is an integral part of life. Work in itself

is doing something useful as well as giving us resources to help those in need.

- Watch the way we talk. Say only what helps. Our words can build people up. Use speech for good, for encouragement. Encouragement is like verbal sunshine. It costs nothing, but it warms hearts and can even changes lives.

- Be gentle. Forgive one another as quickly as God forgives us. God's vision of church is a community of disciples welcoming all, people who especially need forgiveness and a place where forgiveness abounds. The church, to paraphrase Pope Francis, is a field hospital where wounds are healed.

With these five ingredients in our relationships, God can work wonders through us. And the following advice will sustain those relationships:

Take time to think … it's the source of power. Take time to read … it's the fountain of wisdom. Take time to pray … it's the greatest power on earth. Take time to love and be loved … it's a God-given privilege. Laugh … it's the muse of the soul. Take time to work … it's the price of success. And take time to do good things for others … it's the road to happiness and the key to the heavenly banquet.

TWENTY-NINTH SUNDAY
IN ORDINARY TIME

I just reread two amusing stories. A little girl who was attending a wedding whispered to her mother, "Mommy, why is the bride dressed in white?" The mother replied, "Because white is the color of happiness and today is the happiest day of her life." The child paused and then asked, "So why is the groom wearing black?"

The other story is about a boy who asked, "Grandpa, make a sound like a frog." Grandpa answered, "Okay, but why?" The boy said, "Because I heard Mommy and Daddy say as soon as you croak, we're going to Disney World." Yes, be careful what you say around kids.

The word of God carries us back to the sixth century before Jesus (the 500s). Cyrus II, king of Persia (Iran today), conquered Babylonia and set the Jews free so they could return to their homeland to rebuild their temple and Jerusalem. The author proclaimed that there is no God comparable to the God of Israel. He even worked through an unlikely king like Cyrus to achieve his purpose in the history of our salvation (Isa 45:1, 4–6).

The author may be asking us, Do we recognize the presence of God not only in likely people and places but also in the least likely people and places? The Spirit of God breathes wherever it wills.

In his letter to the Christian community at Thessalonica in Greece, Paul prayed that God would continue to grace that community because of their fidelity to the gospel way of life. The living Christ lives and breathes in the community by the power of the Spirit and strengthens them in their faith, hope, and love (1 Thes 1:1–5).

Paul's prayer for the community is ours—that the living Christ would grace us so we may be ever faithful to the gospel way of life.

In the Gospel according to Matthew, the Jews were political prisoners again—this time to the Romans. They had to pay taxes to their oppressors, and even worse, they had to use foreign coinage, which carried the image of the reigning Roman emperor and ascribed divine status to him—blasphemy to the Jews.

The opponents of Jesus posed a tricky question meant to discredit Jesus. Should they pay the tax or not? If Jesus said, "Yes, pay the tax," he would anger his Jewish followers; if he said, "No, don't pay," he would be considered a rebel and liable to death for treason. But Jesus recognized his opponents as hypocrites. So, Jesus answered in a carefully nuanced fashion. If you benefit from Caesar, you ought to pay for the benefits; however, you should give to God what is his by right. The religious leaders knew what Jesus meant. They were to give themselves completely to God since they were made in God's image. We are creatures born to be in relationship with our creator forever (Mt 22:15–21).

An Asian Indian proverb says every one of us is like a house with four rooms—a physical room, a mental room, an emotional room, and a spiritual room. There's even an interesting memoir titled *A House with Four Rooms*. In it are a fully-equipped kitchen; a library with the best books; a studio for painting, pottery, sculpting, and carpentry; and a high-tech room.

Now imagine this scenario. We might become so interested in one room that it becomes the only room we live in. We are so immersed in cooking that we never discover great books; so plugged into high-tech toys that we never sit down to enjoy a dinner; or so engrossed in our work that we don't really connect with the people closest to us.

Some people tend to live most of the time in one room. But unless we go into every room every day, even if it's only to air it out, we are incomplete, not fully alive.

God asks us to throw open every window and door in this so-called house that is our life to allow God's presence to "air out" our physical, mental, emotional, and spiritual aspects. We're not fully alive until the presence of God permeates every dimension of our lives.

In other words, practice the presence of God. The great masters of Christian spirituality say this practice is an art. And where better to develop this practice than in the liturgy?

Yes, the living Christ is present as we gather together in his name. He dwells in each one of us, initially through the waters of baptism and now through a life of discipleship. Moreover, we are all connected to one another through the mystical body of Christ. A warm welcome expresses interconnectedness when we gather.

The living Christ invites us to worship our heavenly Father in the songs we sing, the prayers we pray, and the sacrament we celebrate.

We experience Christ's presence together in the word of God. Yes, we hear the voice of the reader, but it is Christ who is speaking to us. And so we ought to be listening with open ears and open hearts, listening attentively because Christ has a word, perhaps a single word, meant for each of us, a word that hits home.

Foremost, Christ reveals his presence to us sacramentally in his body and blood. Our Catholic tradition teaches us that the bread and wine truly become the reality of the living Christ. How can this be? It is a mystery of our faith. And then Christ offers himself to us as spiritual nourishment in communion. This is a personal and yet a communal moment in which we are united with Christ through his mystical body with all who share this sacred meal worldwide. Communion links us to the mystical body of Christ dwelling within the church universal. This liturgy is a worldwide "community of disciples" experience.

If we can experience the presence of the living Christ as we gather together to worship our heavenly Father, as we listen attentively to the word of God, and as we partake of Christ's body and blood in a communion that unites us to the mystical body of Christ, then we will be able to practice the presence of God more easily in the various imaginary "rooms" of our lives.

Finally, how often do we hear, "How was your day"? I conclude with a story about two parents tucking their children into bed at night and asking that question differently. "Where did you meet God today?" And the children told their parents, one by one, "A teacher helped me; I held the door for someone; I saw a garden with lots of flowers." And the parents told them where they met God too. The stuff of that day became the substance of that family's prayer.

May we be ever more open to the presence of God in the imaginary "rooms of the house" we call our life, and may God's presence permeate every dimension of our lives.

THIRTIETH SUNDAY IN
ORDINARY TIME

You may have heard the story about three health care professionals who died and stood before St. Peter at the pearly gates of heaven.

St. Peter said to the first, "Tell me about what you did on earth." The doctor said, "I did surgery on thousands of patients and improved their lives. "Enter!" said St. Peter. Then the second said, "I was a trauma nurse practitioner. I helped save hundreds of people involved in horrific accidents." "Enter!" signaled St. Peter and turned to the third, who admitted, "I worked for an HMO and saved my company money by refusing care to people trying to use the system." "Enter!" said St. Peter. "You mean it?" the agent asked. "Yes," said St. Peter. "You've been preapproved for only thirty days." Talk about a statement coming back to bite you.

The word of God carries us back in our imaginations to the thirteenth century before Jesus (the 1200s), to the covenant (or special relationship) God renewed with the Hebrews on Mt. Sinai after he freed them from their oppressors in ancient Egypt. The author proclaimed that the covenant was meaningless if the Hebrews didn't treat people compassionately (Ex 22:20–26). The author's words challenge us to treat one another compassionately, especially the vulnerable.

Paul's letter praises the Christians of Thessalonica in Greece as models of discipleship. They, despite all kinds of hardships, continue as faithful disciples of Jesus. Paul may be asking whether we are examples of discipleship for others (1 Thes 1:5–10).

In the Gospel according to Matthew, we picture Jesus surrounded by Pharisees, somewhat like aggressive reporters. A clever lawyer here tried to stump Jesus. "Teacher, which is the great commandment in the law?" A tricky question. Why? Because the law had 613 do's and don'ts. Jesus answered simply by reciting the daily Jewish prayer, the Shema ("Hear!"). "You shall love the Lord your God, with all your heart, and with all your soul, and with all your strength." But then Jesus startled the Pharisees by adding love of one's neighbor. We love God to the extent that we love our fellow human beings (Mt 22:34–40).

We often judge people by appearances: how they look or dress or talk. Here's a true story:

A very ordinary-looking couple went to see the president of Harvard University. The secretary surmised from their scruffy clothes that they had no business at Harvard. "We'd like to see the president," the man said softly. "He's busy all day," she replied. "We'll wait," the woman answered. Finally, the president asked them in. The couple said their son had died a year ago and loved Harvard; they wanted to memorialize him with a building on campus. The surprised president said, "Do you know how much such a building costs? Ten million dollars." He dismissed them. Later the wife said to her husband, "All it costs to start a college is ten million dollars per building." Mr. and Mrs. Leland Stanford headed to California to build Stanford University.

Yes, we often forget. Behind appearances, people reflect the image of God. To be a disciple of Jesus is, first, to see the likeness of God in our fellow humans. Matthew 25 connects love of God with love of our neighbor. "When I was hungry, when I was thirsty" you did something. We can't say we love God and yet neglect our fellow human beings.

How many have heard of Alfred Nobel? He's best known for the Nobel Peace Prize. Less well known is that he was a weapons manufacturer. In 1888, his brother Ludvig died. A French newspaper erroneously published an obituary on *Alfred*, "Le marchand de la mort est mort" (The merchant of death is dead), stating, "Dr. Alfred Nobel, who became rich by finding ways to kill more people faster than ever before, died yesterday." Alfred Nobel was devastated by the "fake news.":

Was this how he would be remembered? Absolutely not! His last will and testament assigned the bulk of his estate to establish the Nobel prizes, for which he is remembered well.

How do we want to be remembered? All of us, as missionary disciples of Jesus, are called to make a difference for the better in the lives of people.

You may remember the play and film *Joseph and the Amazing Technicolor Dreamcoat*. In younger days, wrote the author of Genesis, Joseph went through betrayal by his jealous brothers and then slavery in Egypt. Yet in all these misfortunes, Joseph was ever faithful to God, trusting in God's unconditional love for him. Soon the powerless slave became the powerful administrator in the court of the pharaoh of Egypt, who made Joseph master of *his house*, ruler over all he possessed.

Not only did Joseph remain faithful to God, but he also forgave his brothers for what they had done to him. Ultimately, Joseph's faithfulness to God led to a life of great fruitfulness.

Our lives also should be immensely fruitful, because the Spirit of God lives within us. We are "the temple of the living God," wrote Paul (2 Cor 6:16). Just as God dwelt in the Jerusalem temple, so now he dwells in us by his Spirit. The Spirit produces love, joy, peace, patience, kindness, generosity, faithfulness, gentleness, and self-control (Gal 5:22–23).

St. Paul's life was fruitful. He enriched many (2 Cor 6:10). "Riches" for Paul were the spiritual riches of being in Christ. Paul's life continues to enrich many today, especially in his letters.

Like Joseph, Paul's fruitfulness came at a price. He listed some of the things he endured, including "hardships ... beatings, imprisonments ... slandered ... distrusted ... having nothing" (2 Cor 6:.4–10). Looking at Paul's life puts our own problems into perspective.

In all these hardships, Paul remained faithful to the God who loved him unconditionally. Paul always tried to act with integrity. To act with integrity is to first know who we are, what we stand for, what we believe, and what we care most about. In particular, Paul recognized that we are the temples of the living God, that God lives and moves in us. God is a father to us, and we are his sons and daughters, heirs to the kingdom of God. Therefore, our challenge is to make our lives fit and holy temples for God dwelling in us.

God wants us to be branches in his vine, producing fruit. The Gospel according to John explains, "Jesus is the true vine, and my Father is the vine grower … Remain in me, as I remain in you. Just as a branch cannot bear fruit on its own unless it remains on the vine, so neither can you unless you remain in me. I am the vine, you are the branches" (Jn 15: 1–5).

I close with a paraphrase of one of my favorite sayings: we shall pass through this world but once. Any good therefore that we can do or any kindness that we can show to any human being, let us do it now. Let's not defer or neglect it, for we shall not pass this way again. With this advice embedded into us, our love of God will shine through our love of our fellow human beings.

THIRTY-FIRST SUNDAY
IN ORDINARY TIME

The Gospels often highlight arguments the religious leaders of Judaism had with Jesus.

I read a story, showing how to start a really good argument. A woman wanted a new SUV, something practical; her husband wanted a flashy sports car. After many conversations, he finally said in frustration, "My birthday's in a week, and I want something that goes from zero to two hundred in four seconds or less! Surprise me." So, for his birthday, the woman bought him a bathroom scale. That's when the argument started. The moral of the story? Watch what you say and do; you may start an argument with unintended consequences.

The author of the book of Malachi conveyed his unhappiness with the leadership of Israel in the fifth century BC (the 400s). Yes, the author said, "You have rebuilt the temple," but then scolded these religious leaders for their careless worship, which jeopardized the special relationship (or covenant) God had made with the Hebrews centuries before. But all wasn't lost; God, our Father, never reneges on his promises. He is always faithful despite our unfaithfulness. The point is simple. Act like God's people, always trying to keep promises to God (Mal 1:14–2:2, 8–10).

The author of Malachi may also challenge us to ask, What is leadership? For me, leadership is about three *c*'s: character, courage, and a can-do attitude:

Character defines who we are at our core. It involves ethics, a sense of duty, a value system, morality, and integrity.

Leadership also demands courage—moving beyond our fears and self-doubts to achieve something worthwhile.

Moreover, leadership presumes a positive can-do attitude. Leaders know what they want, why they want it, and how to communicate that to galvanize others into action. They're optimists. They take the initiative, get the facts, have self-confidence, and instill confidence in others.

At different times in life, all of us are called to be leaders—as professionals, business people, parents, citizens, and volunteers. And again, what are the ingredients of leadership? The three c's: character, courage, and a can-do attitude. Think about these ingredients in your leadership roles.

In his letter Paul spoke about his fondness for the Christian community at Thessalonica in Greece. Paul worked hard at his tent-making business so he wouldn't burden them. And then Paul urged them to let the word of God be a guide to life, a message of hope. After all, the only gospel some will ever read are our everyday behaviors and attitudes (1 Thes 2:7–9, 13).

In the Gospel according to Matthew, Jesus condemned the scribes and Pharisees because they said one thing and did another (Mt 23:1–12). They made impossible demands on ordinary people. Worse, they did everything for show. They wanted people to address them with titles. But Jesus said there was only one teacher, Jesus; and only one father, God. Jesus then concluded, "Serve one another. Be the eyes and ears and voice and hands and feet of Christ to other people."

What caught my eye is Paul's reminder to the Thessalonians that God spoke to them in the Bible. Did you ever wonder whether God is speaking to you? In fact, he is. God speaks to us, especially through the inspired word of God, the Bible, a privileged form of conversation between God and us, a two-way conversation. That's why we should be ever attentive to the word of God, especially in the liturgy. God authored the Bible in the sense that the Bible includes what God wants us to know about God, the universe, and ourselves. But the human authors of the Bible were real authors. They employed the language, images, literary genres, and worldviews they knew to communicate religious truths, not scientific truths.

Moreover, the Bible isn't one book but a library. It is made up of prose and poetry, fiction and history, myths and legends, historical narratives and short stories, genealogies and sermons, parables and letters, songs and codes of law, blessings and admonitions, and prophetic and proverbial sayings and apocalyptic visions. Some books in the Bible evolved over decades; others over centuries. In fact, at least forty authors wrote the Bible over fifteen hundred years. They aren't always easily understandable. That why we have Bible study.

The apostle Paul described all scripture as "inspired by God" (2 Tm 3:16), not just inspired in the way artists, poets, composers, and musicians are. Scripture actually has God's breath, his Spirit. Yes, through the Bible, God speaks to us.

The Bible ultimately is about Jesus. Paul informed Timothy that the sacred scriptures are "capable of giving you wisdom for salvation through faith in Christ Jesus" (2 Tm 3:15).

Paul spoke to a society not unlike our own. People, Paul wrote, are going to be self-absorbed, money-hungry, self-promoting, crude, treacherous, ruthless, and bloated windbags and addicts of lust (See 2 Tm 3:1–4). But the followers of Christ are called to be different. "Remain faithful," Paul wrote, "to what you have learned and believed" (2 Tm 3:14).

The temptation is to place our trust and security in money, education, job, health, family, or friends. There's nothing wrong with these things, but ultimately there's only one absolutely secure place in which to put our trust: in Jesus. He loves us unconditionally and asks that we not only hear God's word but also put it into practice.

Our spiritual appetite can be satisfied only in a relationship with God. And that's what Jesus made a reality through his death and resurrection.

Our global Catholic Church is a biblical community of disciples in the sense that it acknowledges and proclaims the Bible as the word of God in human form. In particular, the scriptures point to Jesus as the unique, definitive revelation of God to us. In other words, everything God ever wanted to do for us or say to us, God did and said in Jesus.

In this sense, there will be no new revelation. However, the church universal as a community of disciples is the instrument of the Spirit, who guides us along the journey to eternal life in the light of new problems in new generations and new cultures.

I conclude with a story about Fyodor Dostoyevsky, the great Russian novelist. Many of us have read his *Crime and Punishment* or *The Brothers Karamazov* in high school or college. Dostoyevsky was a wild young man with a lavish lifestyle. Caught up in a movement for political and social reform during the repressive reign of Tsar Nicholas I, he and his comrades were arrested, tried, and condemned to be executed. As the prison guards raised their muskets to their shoulders and took aim, a white flag was raised to announce that the tsar had commuted their sentence to life imprisonment in Siberia.

While in prison, Dostoyevsky read the New Testament from cover to cover and learned much of it by heart. He wrote, "I believe that there is no one ... else like Jesus." Yes, through the Bible, Dostoyevsky encountered the living Christ.

May we also encounter the living Christ in the word of God.

THIRTY-SECOND SUNDAY
IN ORDINARY TIME

So many people today seem to be searching for wisdom in light of global challenges. The early twentieth-century American humorist, actor, and author Will Rogers, for example, noted that we could slow the aging process down if it had to work its way through Congress. Now here's a bit of wisdom I like: "May your troubles be less, may your blessings be more, and may nothing but happiness come through your door." That's my prayer for our veterans.

The book of Wisdom is a collection of sayings about how to live. In today's reading the author personified wisdom as a woman, and wisdom is one with God (Wis 6:12–16). The author challenges us to seek true wisdom, a right relationship with God and our fellow human beings. The living Christ is the source of all wisdom.

The author may be posing the following question to us: do we have our priorities straight? First things first, let's look at our relationships.

In his letter to the Christian community at Thessalonica in Greece, Paul spoke about the triumphant return of Jesus at the end-time. Paul wrote that the resurrection of Jesus is the guarantee of our own resurrection. Yes, we believe, despite the evils on this planet, that good will ultimately triumph with the glorious Second Coming of Jesus and the transformation of our universe into a new heaven and new earth (1 Thes 4:13–18).

In the Gospel according to Matthew, Jesus told a parable or story about preparing to meet God in the mystery of death. The oil can be understood as our good works; the absence of oil is the lack of good works. Seize every opportunity to do good now. Why? Because we don't know the day or hour of our death (Mt 25:1–13). The news every day underscores this truth. People suddenly die in natural disasters, auto crashes, mass shootings, or drug overdoses. Life can be short, so seize every opportunity to do good. "Be prepared" isn't simply a Boy Scout motto. It's an everyday Christian motto.

Today's gospel calls to my mind a medieval fable about a businessman who sent an employee to the Baghdad marketplace. There the employee saw the figure of death. Death seemed to look threateningly at him. He rushed back to his employer and begged for a horse so he could flee. The businessman obliged, and the employee galloped off to the city of Samara. Later, the businessman went to the Baghdad market, and he also saw the figure of death. He asked why death had stared so threateningly at his employee. Death replied, "That was a look of surprise. I was surprised to see him in Baghdad. You see, I have an appointment with him in the city of Samara tonight."

This fable reinforces the theme of watchfulness or readiness. Are we ready to meet God in the mystery of death? If not today, when will we be ready? What do we have to do today to be ready? We know there are some things we can do to delay death. We can exercise and eat the right foods. We can stop smoking and so on. But there's a basic truth. We ultimately will have to keep an appointment with death sometime, someday, some year. But the good news is this. As people of faith, we know that the God who gave us life will transform our earthly selves into new, indescribable heavenly selves. That's the Easter message.

So how do we prepare to meet God? First, we should value each day as a gift from God and live today as best we can. Make every day worth living.

Emerging medical technologies may soon be able to lengthen our years into the hundreds. But the underlying question remains. Will it still be worth living? An increase in lifespan is of little value unless it's a life of quality. Interestingly a surgeon, Atul Gawande, wrote a best seller titled *Being Mortal*. It's a narrative about the care and treatment of the elderly and the dying as care evolved over the last century to what it is today and could become tomorrow. Gawande questions whether employing technologies to lengthen a life at the expense of a quality life is the right thing to do. The question becomes when to let go, when to stop treatments that likely don't work. Gawande asks, "Why submit the dying to the full panoply of procedures only to see them merely exist in institutions and lose their independence?" After all, birth and death are both integral to the cycle of life.

St. Paul didn't see prolonging life as a major goal; he wrote to the Philippians, "For me, life is Christ, and death is gain" (Phil 1:21). Indeed, Paul saw death as of greater worth. Yet Jesus made Paul's life profoundly worth living.

We were created to live in a relationship with God through Jesus Christ by the power of the Spirit. Without that relationship, we will feel empty deep inside. As St. Augustine wrote, "God, you have made us for yourself and our hearts are restless until they rest in you." Yes, no matter who we are or what we do, our true purpose is to be in relationship with God. That's what makes life worth living.

People try to fill their emptiness with different things. For some, it's alcohol, money, status, or so-called expensive toys. For St. Paul, a life worth living is knowing Christ "in whom are hidden *all the treasures of wisdom*" (Col 2:2–3).

Let's face it. Sometimes don't we wish our circumstances were different? Yet even when we're facing out-of-the-blue challenges, we should be confident that God can and does work through us in ways we may not expect. When St. Paul, for example, wrote his letter to the Philippians, he was a prisoner awaiting trial and possible execution. Yet he believed God could work in him, even then and there. Pray, like St. Paul, that we may be holy both inwardly and outwardly. Dietrich Bonhoeffer, the theologian who was executed for standing up against Nazism, put it well. "Your life as a Christian should make nonbelievers question their disbelief in God."

Paul's life was centered on Christ. His desire was for Christ to "be magnified in his body, whether by life or by death" (Phil 1:20). Though Paul longed to be with Christ, part of him also wanted to stay alive because he knew it would mean "fruitful labor" for Christ. Paul took every opportunity, no matter the circumstances, to spread the gospel, the good news. He was a missionary disciple.

We are also called to be missionary disciples, to do the right thing, to make our lives worth living. You've heard the saying "Cowardice asks the question, Is it safe? Expediency asks, Is it politic? Vanity asks, Is it popular? But, conscience asks, Is it right?"

Yes, many times in life, the first question we must ask is, What is the right thing to do? And then just do it. Then our "lamps" will be filled with the oil of good works when we meet God in the mystery of death.

THIRTY-THIRD SUNDAY
IN ORDINARY TIME

A cross this great land of ours, on Thursday families will gather to celebrate Thanksgiving to give thanks to God for our life, talents, family and friends, and opportunities to become our best selves. The rousing hymn "America the Beautiful" is a fitting Thanksgiving tribute.

The holidays are here, and ads are everywhere about staying young. Here's my advice: Hang around happy people. Avoid complainers. Keep learning. Enjoy the simple things. Laugh often. Grieve, yes; but then move on. Surround yourself with what you love—family, pets, and hobbies. Tell the people you love that you love them at every opportunity.

Above all, tune into the presence of God every day through prayer. God is closer to us than we are to ourselves. That's good holiday advice.

The word of God carries us back to the wisdom literature of ancient Israel in the book of Proverbs. The author described the ideal wife in second-century Judaism. She was more precious than diamonds, trusted by her husband, and blessed by her children. She was a person of her word, a good housewife and a savvy businesswoman, always ready to help the needy. Above all, she lived in awe of God, who loves us unconditionally (Pr 31:10–13, 19–20, 30–31).

The author may be asking us, Do we keep our word? Do we live in awe of our Creator God?

From Paul we have a passionate exhortation to stay awake, not to be caught by surprise when Christ comes. It's an exhortation that makes sense only if we're convinced Armageddon is right around the corner. Paul urged us to live as children of light, to become godlike in our everyday behavior (1 Thes 5:1–6).

From Jesus we have a parable of a wealthy man, about to travel, who gives money to each of his three servants according to their abilities. On his return, he asks what they did with the money. The first two doubled theirs bullishly. The third didn't take any risks; he simply buried the money (Mt 25:14–30).

The parable challenges us to ask, Which servant are we? Are we using our talents as best we can for others, like the first and second servants? Or are we squandering them?

The overriding theme of the ideal wife in Proverbs, of Paul in his letter, and of Jesus in the gospel is faithfulness. All three were faithful, full of faith. So what is faith? The letter to the Hebrews says faith is "the realization of what is hoped for and evidence of things not seen" (Heb 11:1).

Some of you may remember the Rolling Stones song "(I Can't Get No) Satisfaction." That line echoes the cry of the human heart; we try, and we try, but we're never satisfied. True satisfaction comes through faith in Jesus Christ, who said, "I came so that you may have life, and have it more abundantly" (Jn 10:10). Faith, a gift from God, empowers us to have a relationship with God.

What does faith look like in practice? The biblical Abraham is a model of faith in God. There are at least three ingredients:

- Faith trusts in God's unconditional love for us. It's saying yes to God. Abraham said yes to God's call to travel to an unknown place that would become his home. He heard God's call and obeyed. He didn't know where he was going, but he knew with whom he was traveling—with God. And his leap of faith brought him blessings. Abraham trusted God, even when evidence pointed otherwise. His great disappointment was that his wife couldn't have children (Heb 11:12). But Abraham believed in the power of God despite his doubts. And God blessed them with a son, Isaac.

- Faith sees beyond this earthly life. We live in an instant culture. Everything is about instant satisfaction. But Abraham was in life for the long haul. He was a stranger in a foreign country. He lived in tents. Yet he didn't look back once he had made his initial leap of faith into the unknown. Rather, "he was looking forward to the city with foundations, whose architect and maker is God" (Heb 11:10).

- Faith is staying faithful to God despite doubts to the contrary. Forgetfulness of God is the opposite of faith. Faith is keeping our eyes fixed on God, trusting in him, abiding with him, and serving him with all our hearts. It's staying faithful despite the challenges we face, no matter how overwhelming they may appear.

We are by nature believers. Think about the ordinary things we do. We turn on the ignition key and expect the car to start. We turn on the house lights and expect light. If you think about it, we live by faith.

Our Catholic faith is a gift from God that empowers us to have a right relationship with the triune God as creator, redeemer, and sanctifier.

Faith is richer and deeper than belief. Faith invites us to enter an encounter with the living Christ, to follow him, who is our way to eternal life; our truth, who sets us free from falsehoods; and our light, who illuminates the darkness around us as we journey toward our heavenly dwelling place. Faith is about connectedness to the triune God … It's about our relationship with God that we nurture especially through prayer.

Belief, on the other hand, is a statement about the essential truths of our faith we will proclaim shortly in our fourth-century Nicene Creed.

We say, "I believe in one God," despite many folks today who experience not the presence but the absence of God. They question the existence of God in the face of such overwhelming evils as disease, senseless violence, war, and hunger.

Yes, we say, our God is almighty, the maker of heaven and earth, of everything visible and invisible. We profess there is an awesome power completely other and completely beyond ourselves. There is One who is the cause and is responsible for everything that is: God, Father Almighty.

And yes, we believe in one lord, Jesus Christ. Jesus Christ, for us and for our salvation, came down from heaven. Today there is so much brokenness on this planet; something isn't quite right. There are hate, lies, injustice, greed, the denial of human rights, ignorance, and violence. This planet cries out for a healer, a reconciler. And this Jesus who for our sake was crucified, died, was buried, and rose again is our one healer, our one reconciler, and our one pledge of a life beyond this earthly life.

Yes, we believe in the Holy Spirit, the Lord, the giver of life. The power and gifts of the Spirit are within us. And they enable us to take charge of our destiny and do good for others.

We believe in one, holy, catholic, and apostolic community. We acknowledge one baptism and look to the resurrection and the life to come.

This creed underscores the essential content of faith; what we believe truly matters.

May the God who loves us unconditionally increase our faith so we can see what lies beneath and beyond immediate appearances—that is, the presence of God all around us. And may that experience inspire us to live a godlike life.

THE FEAST OF CHRIST THE KING

I really enjoy Thanksgiving. No gifts to buy, no lights to hang, no tree to decorate. It's all about family enjoying one another's company. And telling stories. Here's one I heard.

A dad was trying to get the ketchup out of a bottle, and he was hitting it on the kitchen table. The phone rang, so he asked his four-year-old to answer the phone. The child said, "Daddy can't come to the phone right now. He's hitting the bottle."

Yes, children can say the darndest things.

Today we celebrate the Feast of Christ, the King, which closes the liturgical year. It is a history of our salvation beginning with hope in Advent, moving to the Messiah's birth at Christmas, continuing through Lent into the Easter triduum and Pentecost, and then proceeding throughout ordinary time and culminating in the Second Coming of Christ in glory in today's gospel.

Liturgically, we have reached the end of salvation history, when every human being and all that is will be subjected to Christ, "who will deliver the kingdom of God over to his heavenly Father" (1 Cor 15:28). Yes, Jesus Christ is our King, to whom we owe our ultimate allegiance.

Pope Pius XI created this feast in 1925 in the aftermath of World War I, a bloody conflict which toppled thrones in Germany, Russia, Austria, and Turkey. The purpose of the feast was to reunite all of us in a higher allegiance.

The word of God today carries us in our imaginations to the sixth century before Jesus (the 500s). The author here criticized the kings of Judah—wicked and false shepherds, he wrote—and described the Hebrews as lost, injured, and sick. And in describing their circumstances, the author may have been describing our own (Eze 34:11–12, 15–17).

The author of Ezekiel wondered aloud whether there was a power beyond us who could set things right. Yes, who can set things right for us? Jesus of Nazareth, once dead and now alive, who seeks the lost, cares for the injured, and heals the sick. Yes, the One who reestablishes our relationship with God and our fellow human beings.

In his letter to the Christian community at Corinth, Paul spoke about life and death, good and evil, and the Parousia or the triumphant return of Jesus at the end-time. Then the Son will hand over the kingdom to the Father (1 Cor 15:20–26, 28).

In the meantime, we are called to be cocreators, co-stewards, and coworkers with God in ushering in that kingdom. In particular, we are called on to build here and now a social order founded on truth, justice, love, and freedom.

In the Gospel according to Matthew, the author described the final roundup in the parable of the sheep and goats, the parable about judgment (Mt 25:31–46).

How will God judge us? By how we treat one another. In people, we encounter God. Love of God is inseparable from love of our fellow human beings.

Today I would like to take my cue from St. Paul's letter. Many people today cry out for freedom from tyrannies that dehumanize them. All we must do is tune into the news. So many people beg for a livable, viable social order built on truth, justice, love, and freedom.

Truth is a powerful word in our Catholic heritage. What we say ought to be in sync with what really is. Lies undermine trust in one another. Truth can't mean one thing for one person and the opposite for another person. Yes, truth is an essential ingredient in a Christian social order and in our relationships. To be severed from what's true is to be severed from what's real.

Justice is a second powerful word. Give everyone his or her due. Communities—whether economic, political, national, or international— have rights and duties. At times, we stress duties at the expense of rights or vice versa. But there is no question about it. Justice is an essential ingredient in a Christian social order and in our relationships with one another. To treat others unfairly, to refuse another what is his or her due, is an injustice.

A third powerful word in our Catholic heritage is *love*. Love recognizes that every human being is made in the image of God and reflects the likeness of God, no matter how shabby the appearances. Love compels us to go out of ourselves to others, and in reaching out to others, we reach up to the Other, God himself, who loves us unconditionally. Unfortunately, many limit their love to their own color, country, creed, or "own kind." Yes, love is essential in a Christian social order and in our relationships. Love gives hope to many who might otherwise despair. It's wishing the other person well and helping the other, if we can, to become his or her best self.

A fourth powerful word is *freedom*. The word has two facets: freedom from and freedom for. What we have been freed from is always some form of oppression or tyranny. The thirteen US colonies, for example, rebelled against Britain—against what the colonists saw as abuses of their rights and liberties. The civil rights movement protested a social system that condemned blacks to the back of a bus in certain states, forbade them a pew in particular churches, and barred them from specific restaurants simply because of color.

Christianity is all about freedom. God became one of us in Jesus to free us from all that keeps us from a relationship with God, one another, and the universe.

Yes, to be freed from something is only one side of the coin. We have been freed *from* something so we can be free *for* something. St. Paul wrote to the Galatians, "You were called to freedom … to be servants." Yes, we are free so we can serve.

All around us are people who are hungry for bread, peace, human rights, and justice. Only a social order based on truth, justice, love, and freedom can satisfy these hungers. Such a social order frees us to become our true selves, human beings in authentic relationships with God and one another.

I close with a scene from a true story that appeared in a newspaper. A homeless man was sitting on the curb. He had set his hat out. A homeless woman, walking by, paused. Deciding that he was worse off than she, the so-called bag lady took from her worn, ripped coat pocket two crumpled dollar bills and placed them in his hat.

It's a random act of kindness, almost unnoticed, but a snapshot of compassion that both inspired the spirit and broke the heart.

So often we too would like to help, but it sometimes seems to be at a bad time. But the woman put aside her own hardships at a bad time to compassionately reach out to someone. That is holiness; that's discipleship.

Christ the Shepherd-King calls us to embrace his mind-set, to realize that among the many blessings we have from God is the gift to share what we have with others.

In doing so, we are building the kingdom of God, a kingdom of truth, justice, love, and freedom. And for that blessing may we be truly thankful.

THE EPIPHANY OF THE LORD

I was in New York City over the Christmas holidays and sitting in the foyer of a hotel, waiting for a friend. A woman sat down on a sofa opposite mine. She was wearing a huge diamond ring. Curiosity got the better of me, and I asked, "Pardon me, ma'am, but the ring you're wearing … I've never seen a gem that large. What is it?" She said, "It's the Smith diamond, named for my husband; it's like the Hope diamond. It comes with a downside." And I said, "What's the downside?" "Mr. Smith." So much for diamonds.

The holidays are over. We're ready to get back to work, and perhaps we have made a few resolutions for the New Year. This year I didn't make any. How about you? There are books, for example, I always thought I should read and never have; I'm not going to read them this year either. There may be a day when I miss reading the newspaper, too, and I'm not going to kid myself this year. So if I haven't read today's newspaper by tomorrow, I'm throwing it out. I'm giving up on resolutions in 2017.

Today we celebrate the Epiphany or the manifestation or showing forth of the child Jesus as the Messiah to the magi. We really don't know who these visitors were—wise men, astrologers, or spice traders. All we know is that they were non-Jews who came from far away, guided by a mysterious star, to pay homage to this Jewish baby called Jesus.

The word of God from Isaiah takes us back in our imaginations to the sixth century before Jesus, the 500s. The sixth century was catastrophic for the Jews. They lost everything they thought would continue forever, including Jerusalem, the temple, and the monarchy.

Fr. Kevin E. Mackin, OFM

Ancient Babylonia conquered Jerusalem, razed the temple to the ground, eliminated the monarchy, and deported many Jews to Babylonia. But then Persia conquered Babylonia and set the Jews free to rebuild their city. In this passage, the author referred to a new Jerusalem. A divine light would emanate from this shining city on a hill, and all people, Jews as well as non-Jews, would acknowledge and walk by this light (Isa 60:1–6).

Christians see Jesus as this light who illuminates darkness, the light who shows human beings the ultimate purpose of life—to be in relationship with God and thereby manifest the glory of God through who we are and what we do.

Paul's letter to the Christian community at Ephesus in Turkey outlines our future. We are coheirs to the kingdom of God and coworkers of Jesus in bringing about the fullness of the kingdom (Eph 3:2–3, 5–6). Jesus is indeed our guide in this work, a path to the lost, a loaf of bread to the spiritually hungry, an arm for the weak, a companion to the lonely, and a beacon of hope for all.

In the Gospel according to Matthew, we have all the ingredients of a great story: exotic visitors, a wicked king, court intrigue, a mysterious star, precious gifts, and a new child. The magi gave homage to this child with gifts of gold, frankincense, and myrrh. They were highly symbolic gifts about the identity of this child (Mt 2:1–12).

Gold can symbolize kingship or divinity, the things of God; and the "coins" of this child's heavenly realm are the virtues of self-discipline, compassion, responsibility, friendship, courage, perseverance, honesty, decency, respect, and faith in God. Are these virtues the currency of our own lives?

Frankincense, with its wonderful fragrance and medicinal magic, can symbolize healing, and this child came to heal our wounds and bridge the chasm that separates us from God and one another. We too are called to be healers to one another.

Myrrh or ointment can symbolize a burial embalmment, and this child through his dying and rising reestablished our relationship with God and made us coheirs to God's promise of eternal life.

Now who is this child to whom the magi give their homage? This newborn Messiah, soon to grow into the adult Messiah, completely human and completely divine, is the exemplar, prototype, or model of what it means to be an authentic human being. That is why some ask themselves as they go about their daily routine, "What would Jesus do in this or that circumstance?"

With Jesus—his life, ministry, dying, and rising—as our model, God invites us from an infinite number of possibilities to become the best version of ourselves.

But what is that? In other words, what is our essential purpose? We are called to be in relationship with God by living holy lives, every man and woman, without exception, regardless of our age, color, socioeconomic background, career, or calling in life.

Holiness is allowing God to enter every part of our lives so we can become the best version of ourselves through who we are and everything we do. It's trying to be true to our inner best selves; it's a willingness to go the extra mile to make something "just right" because it's the better thing to do; it's striving to choose what's the right thing to do in all our decisions, small and great, that affect our work, career, family, social life, the rearing of children, relationships with others, and yes, even our leisure time.

Yes, with Jesus as our model while trying to become the best version of ourselves, now is the time to renew ourselves spiritually as we begin anew.

A wise Middle Eastern mystic said this about himself:

> I was a revolutionary when I was young, and my prayer to God was, "Lord, give me the energy to change the world." As I approached middle age and realized my life was half gone without my changing a single soul, I changed my prayer to "Lord, give me the grace to change all those who come into contact with me. Just my family and friends and I will be satisfied." Now that I am an old man and my days are numbered, I have begun to see how foolish I have been. My one prayer now is: "Lord, give me the grace to change myself, to become the best version of myself." If I had prayed this right from the start, I would not have wasted my life.

Fr. Kevin E. Mackin, OFM

Now is indeed a time to change ourselves, recreate ourselves, and reenergize our lives with God and with one another. It's time to try to become the best version of ourselves.

How? I like this simple suggestion. Each day do a bit more than we think we can.

Each day love a little bit more than we think we can; forgive a little bit more than we think we can; reach out to someone who is hurting a little bit more; sacrifice for others a little bit more; and encourage one another, especially our families, a little bit more than we think we can.

So I do have a New Year's resolution.

And God will give us strength to do more than we think we can.

And if we do a little bit more than we think we can each day, then when our earthly life ends, we will approach God a little bit more closely than we thought we could.

FEAST OF ST. PETER AND ST. PAUL

I read about a senior citizen who bought a new Corvette convertible, drove it onto I-95 North, and quickly was speeding at one hundred miles per hour. In his rearview mirror, he saw a state trooper, blue lights flashing and siren blaring. The man floored the pedal to 110 miles per hour, then 120. Suddenly he thought, *What am I doing? Juvenile behavior!* And he pulled over.

Pulling in behind him, the trooper walked up and said, "Sir, my shift ends in thirty minutes, and it's Friday. If you can give me a reason for speeding—a reason I've never heard—I'll let you go."

The driver paused and said, "Three years ago, my wife ran off with a state trooper, and I thought you were trying to bring her back to me."

"Have a good day, sir," replied the trooper. Creative thinking!

On July 4, we celebrate the signing of the Declaration of Independence in 1776. That document proclaims very simply yet profoundly, "We hold these truths to be self-evident, that all men are created equal, that they are endowed by their Creator with certain unalienable rights, that among these are life, liberty and the pursuit of happiness, that to secure these rights, governments are instituted among men, deriving their powers from the consent of the governed."

We might rededicate ourselves afresh to these principles for people everywhere. These principles are the unfinished business and source of our nation's greatest strength.

Today we celebrate the Feast of Saints Peter and Paul, two ordinary people who did extraordinary things, who stood up for what they believed and died for what they believed. Peter, the rock and the leader, was often spontaneous but always ready to admit a mistake and make amends. He was someone you could trust. And Paul, the preacher, the apostle to the Gentiles, was often argumentative but always courageous in speaking the truth despite the consequences. Perhaps we see some of ourselves in these two ordinary people; transformed into heroes, they were pillars of Christianity by the Spirit of God. We might ask, Who are our own heroes and heroines? Do they symbolize virtues, such as self-discipline, honesty, integrity, responsibility, friendship, courage, perseverance, compassion, loyalty, faith in God, and respect for people? Or something else?

The Acts of the Apostles recounts the miraculous escape of Peter from prison. King Herod imprisoned Peter—not because Peter had committed a crime but because Herod was trying to win the favor of the Jewish leadership by harassing Christians (Acts 12:1–11).

Peter's imprisonment and martyrdom are reminders of the sacrifices he made to be a faithful disciple of Jesus. He knew the cost of discipleship and was willing to pay the price, even death. The question for us is, Are we willing to stand up for what is right, true, and good despite possible consequences?

Paul wrote a very personal letter from prison to his friend Timothy. Paul reflected on his life as he prepared for his death. And he used the image of a race to sum up his life. He had competed well, almost arriving at the finish line; he had been faithful to Jesus and praised God (2 Tm 4:6–8, 17–18). The questions for us are, Can we say the same? Have we done well and kept the faith?

And in the Gospel according to Matthew, Jesus asked Peter, "Who do you say I am?" This is the most important question in the Gospels. Peter answered, "You are the messiah or the anointed One, the fulfillment of the hopes of Ancient Israel" (Mt 16:13–19).

Who do we say Jesus is? What does Jesus mean to us? What did he mean to the early Christian community?

The early Christians saw Jesus as the fulfillment of the hopes of ancient Israel. So they called him the Messiah, the anointed one. The more they reflected on who he was, the more they saw Jesus not only as the fulfillment of their hopes but also the foundation of these hopes as well.

So they named him the eternal Word. The prologue of the Gospel according to John captures this idea magnificently. "In the beginning was the Word and the Word was with God and the Word was God. And the Word became flesh and made his dwelling among us." Yes, Jesus was both the foundation and fulfillment of their hopes as well as our own.

Jesus was a real historical person, flesh and blood like ourselves. He experienced, as we do, fatigue, hunger, satisfaction, joy, friendship, disappointment, and loneliness. He was a rabbi, teacher, and prophet, who preached that the kingdom of God was breaking into our midst. He worked signs and wonders that proclaimed that good ultimately would triumph over evil. He possessed authority to forgive wrongdoings, and he promised eternal life. He had a unique relationship with the God of ancient Israel. He was one with God, but he was crucified and then raised up from the dead. He was transformed into a new heavenly reality; he is alive in our midst today by the power of the Spirit, especially in the sacramental life.

In fact, the risen Christ is alive wherever we are gathered in his name, as we are gathered in his name today; and we too are alive with his grace and favor. And one day, we also will be transformed into a new heavenly reality just as Jesus was before us.

Jesus taught not only that the kingdom of God was breaking into our midst but also that you and I can share in this kingdom of God by living out lives of discipleship. And how is that possible? By living prayerfully in the presence of God; by recognizing that our lives do have an ultimate purpose; by seeing in Jesus—the Word made flesh—the face of God; by reaching out compassionately, especially with our time and talents, to the people around us; by experiencing God's presence in the sacramental life of the community; and by always being ready to let go of our earthly lives in the mystery of death so we can be one with God forever.

Ultimately Jesus taught that God is our Father, a compassionate God, always near at the start of each day to guide us on our way to our heavenly home. Jesus asks you and me, "Who do you say I am?" The answer should shape our lives accordingly.

I will close with a story about a violinist who tripped and fell as he went on stage to play for a special concert. He almost went into shock when his priceless Stradivarius broke into several pieces. But a master craftsman spent hours putting it back together. And afterward, the violin seemed to sound better than before.

Sometimes our lives can break. Jesus invites us to pick up the pieces and let the Master, Jesus Christ, put our lives back together so we, like Peter and Paul, can stand up for what is true as compassionate human beings, men and women of daily prayer and intimacy with God, and above all people who find in Jesus, crucified and risen, the ultimate meaning of life.

EXALTATION OF THE HOLY CROSS

Archbishop Fulton Sheen was scheduled to speak at the town hall in Philadelphia and decided to walk from his hotel to the town hall. He got lost, and he stopped some teenagers to ask for directions, which they happily gave him. Then one of the teens asked Sheen, "What are you going to do at the town hall?" Sheen replied, "I'm giving a lecture." "About what?" asked the teen. "On how to get to heaven. Do you want to come along?" asked Sheen. The teen said, "Are you kidding? You don't even know how to get to the town hall." So much for that.

Some universities have an event inviting faculty to give what's called the "Last Lecture." It's the wisdom a professor would communicate to students if it was his or her last chance. At Carnegie Mellon University, Randy Pausch, a computer science professor, accepted the challenge. But there was one difference. This really was his last lecture. He had just been diagnosed with pancreatic cancer and had less than a year to live.

The lecture about his life was humorous, emotional, and thoughtful. He spoke about the importance of honesty and truth, of perseverance, gratitude, and passion in the pursuit of our dreams. Good things tend to happen, he noted, when you try to do the right thing. People generally show their good side if you're patient enough, and there's no substitute for hard work. He spoke about his love for his family. He described how he had managed to scale the brick walls that stood in the way of achieving some of his dreams.

Above all, in the time left to him, the most important thing was his family.

Did you ever wonder what you would write if asked to give a "Last Lecture"? Especially if it really was your last lecture toward the end of your life? What would you write for your loved ones, children, grandchildren, colleagues, and friends? The lecture would tell you what you prized most in life, which virtues you tried to live, and how you found purpose in life.

I don't expect you to write this lecture this weekend, but I hope you're thinking about it. It's a good tool that can motivate us to try to put our lives together better, so to speak.

The Exaltation of the Holy Cross, today's feast, was indeed Jesus's last lecture to humankind. It wasn't done on paper but on wood.

This feast we celebrate commemorates the finding of the cross in the fourth century Jerusalem by St. Helena, the mother of the emperor Constantine. The cross is the symbol of Christianity. The cross was once a Roman device for executing criminals, often by suffocation. The surgeon Pierre Barbet, in his classic book, *A Doctor at Calvary*, graphically described death by crucifixion in Roman times.

Yet the cross is now a symbol of the triumph of life over death. Why? Because hidden in the tragedy of Good Friday is the triumph of the Easter resurrection.

Now the word of God proclaimed today takes us back in our imaginations over three thousand years to the wanderings of the Hebrews in the Sinai wilderness after their exodus or liberation from ancient Egypt. And here the Hebrews were complaining about their lives. In particular, poisonous snakes were everywhere in this wilderness. God heard the prayer of Moses for his people, and Moses made a pole with an image of a snake on top. And all who looked at the pole lived; this is a Christian allusion to the saving power of the cross (Nm 21).

The passage from the letter of Paul to the Christian community at Philippi in Greece is a thrilling hymn about the tragedy of the cross and the triumph of the resurrection. It is a paradox, tragedy, and triumph all in one (2 Tm 4:6–8, 17–18).

Paul sang that Jesus, though one in glory with the Father, became a weak human being. Jesus learned how to totter and talk as a child. He studied Joseph's trade, felt hunger and joy, wept, got so tired he fell asleep in a boat during a storm, feared death, and died in an indescribable agony. Jesus didn't cling to the glory he had with his Father. He emptied himself of his glory. It's a profoundly theological hymn that captures the central truth of our faith.

And in the Gospel according to John, Jesus compared the image of the serpent lifted in the wilderness to the image of Jesus himself lifted on the cross. Just as that prior image of the serpent in the wilderness healed, so too Jesus, lifted high on the cross, healed humankind and bestowed on you and me God's favor, his eternal life. Yes, out of Jesus's death came God's eternal glory. Jesus is indeed our Savior (Mt 16:13–19).

But think about it: What do we really want to be saved from today?

We live in a culture that advertises countless phony forms of salvation. Madison Avenue advertises everything from expensive cosmetic surgery to the latest drugs. Yes, these will save us—from old age, anxiety, obesity, pain, illness, or whatever. We will look and feel better if we only do this or take that.

But St. Paul put it best. Salvation means we possess within our fragile human selves the gift of God's life by virtue of the death and resurrection of Jesus.

Paul used several words to describe salvation: liberation, justification, or "having a right relationship with God." That was salvation for Paul and the gift of God's life within us.

Salvation is really a process, not a quick fix that happens in an instant. We continually must struggle against the dark side of human life. So salvation isn't a single event but rather a life process that culminates with life with God forever. In other words, life, not death, is what human life is all about.

The word *salvation* tries to answer a fundamental question—what is the ultimate purpose of my life? Whether we are powerful or powerless, rich or poor, no matter our intellect, no matter our national origin— the purpose of life is to be in relationship with God. That's why we are here—to be in relationship or friendship with God forever.

The Catholic answer to the question "Why are we here?" acknowledges the brevity of human life.

It also acknowledges our freedom to choose good over evil, right over wrong, the true over the false. Hence, all of us are responsible or accountable for the way we choose to live. Tragically, people in fact do choose evil sometimes, because there's something not quite right with us. The Catholic tradition calls this "original sin."

Yes, things are definitely not quite right today. In fact, things seem to be a mess in many ways. Soldiers are creating havoc in the eastern Ukraine, jihadists are terrorizing innocent people, and regions are unstable. Yes, there's plenty wrong in this universe of ours; there's plenty wrong with people. Human beings cry out for freedom, peace, justice, and truth. They cry out for salvation.

But who can save us? Some, of course, have sought human solutions to human problems. They have looked for answers in the world of things, in other persons, and in the great "isms" of the twentieth century.

The Catholic tradition looks beyond the world of things to a power beyond ourselves.

This overwhelming power beyond ourselves—God—isn't indifferent to our human situation, for our God is a gracious God. This gracious power beyond ourselves became flesh in Jesus of Nazareth and is alive by the power of the Spirit in our midst today—alive especially in the sacramental life of the church, the community of disciples, with water, bread and wine, and oil.

Yes, we possess within our fragile selves the treasure of God's life. We are in relationship with God. But we must continue to struggle, as the prophet Micah said centuries ago, to do the right, love goodness, and walk humbly with our God.

Salvation, like the words "healing," "made whole," "wellness," and "restoring to right order," describes an overwhelming good, a good beyond our wildest imaginations. That is God's life within us forever. That's what salvation means. That's what the cross signifies.

And I pray that, whenever you see the cross, the central symbol of Christianity, you will remember the purpose of your own life: to be in relationship with God here and hereafter.

ALL SOULS' DAY

Thinking about All Souls' Day, when we celebrate family through the ages, I read that a teenager asked his father when he could begin driving the family car. His father replied, "Bring your grades up to a B average, study your Bible, and get your hair cut. Then we'll talk." The teen agreed to the deal.

After about six weeks the father said, "You've brought your grades up, and you've been studying, but you haven't had your hair cut." His son noted, "In the Bible Samson had long hair, so did John the Baptist, and Moses, and there's strong evidence that Jesus had long hair." His father responded, "Did you also notice they walked everywhere?" No cars in ancient Israel.

The word of God proclaimed today takes us back to the wisdom literature of ancient Israel, about how to deal with the basic questions of life: our quest for happiness, the mystery of suffering, the problem of good and evil, wisdom and folly.

In the second century before Jesus, the author wrote to edify his fellow Jews, who were suffering hardships. The faithful will experience immortality, be blessed, and shine like "sparks." They will possess grace and mercy. The author's words invite us to pray that our deceased loved ones will experience life eternal with God (Wis 3:1–9).

In his letter to the Christian community in Rome, Paul proclaimed that hope triumphs over despair, because Jesus, crucified and risen and in our midst by the power of the Spirit, has reestablished our friendship with God. Paul challenged us to hope in the future, in eternal life (Rom 5:5–11; 6:3–9).

And in the Gospel according to John, Jesus worked seven signs that reveal his identity as the Son of God. Those who live as sons and daughters of God will have eternal life (Jn 6:37–40).

Considering our remembrance of the faithful departed, I would like to look forward. Many are fascinated with the future, especially life after this earthly life. There are books about near-death experiences. Check Amazon.com. They include Dr. Alexander's *Proof of Heaven*, Betty Eadie's *Embraced by the Light*, Elizabeth Kubler-Ross's *Life after Death*, and Raymond Moody's *Life After Life*.

Moody, for example, describes common elements in near-death experiences. People felt themselves moving out of their physical bodies; they heard people trying to resuscitate them; and they felt themselves moving rapidly through a long, dark tunnel into the presence of an overpowering light, which asked them to evaluate their lives. They found themselves hovering on the border between this life and the next—and then being pulled back into their earthly selves.

Moody's book raises many questions. Did these people actually die? Were they "clinically dead"? Some experts say these people weren't describing their deaths as much as a new and deeper experience of human consciousness.

The point is, people are fascinated with the future. What will the future be like? Everywhere we see change—political, economic, scientific, and religious.

In his influential best seller *The World Is Flat: A Brief History of the 21st Century*, Thomas Friedman reminds us that, whether we like it or not, whether we want it or not, the world is stretching our inclusiveness circle, making it bigger. The Internet, cell phones, laptops, tablets, and other technological advances can put us in touch with people from all over the world in seconds. Everywhere we see change—sometimes for the better and sometimes for the worse.

The Bible captures the ambivalence of change magnificently. There is time for everything under the sun—a time to be born, a time to die, and so forth.

People want to know what will happen before it actually happens.

If we find all this bothersome, we do have one consolation. More often than not, forecasters are wrong.

Our own history of Western civilization bears this out. In the fifteenth century, advisers to Ferdinand and Isabella of Spain said that a westerly voyage to the Indies was impossible. Voilà—America was discovered.

In 1784, a French mathematician and philosopher predicted that there would be fewer and fewer revolutions. Lo and behold, he found out how dead wrong he was when he died ten years later in the French reign of terror.

Sometimes we may not like the future unfolding before us, with jihadists, Ebola, shooting sprees, crime, civil wars, economic uncertainties, and so forth.

At times, we seem to be our own worst enemies. We have freed ourselves from so many tyrannies of the past only to create new problems. How should we react? Some rebel, others despair, and still others withdraw.

But what is the Christian response to the shape of the future?

Hope.

Hope is a fundamental human characteristic. We are forever seeking to go beyond the here and now, to dream the impossible dream. We want to reach beyond ourselves for what is yet to come. Hope best expresses what human existence is all about.

There are images of hope weaving in and out of the Hebrew and Christian scriptures. Initially, the hopes of the ancient Hebrews were very concrete. They included land, sons and daughters, peace and prosperity. God was always faithful despite their unfaithfulness.

And when the hopes of the Hebrews were dashed with the fall of the southern kingdom in the sixth century, God began to build up new and better hopes for them—a messianic era, a Messiah who would rescue them from all enemies, even the enemy of death.

The New Testament is rooted and grounded in Jesus of Nazareth. Jesus is our hope.

At the very core of Christianity is the central reality that Jesus appeared alive to the disciples after his death. The tomb was empty. There were many appearances.

God by the power of the Spirit transformed the earthly Jesus into a heavenly Jesus.

And one day we, like Jesus, will make an evolutionary leap into a new reality. By virtue of baptism, we experience the beginnings of that future—life with God forever.

Christian hope is the conviction that the universe has ultimate meaning, that Christ in his Second Coming will bring to completion the process of transformation begun in his resurrection.

This hope challenges us to do everything we can to usher in that future—to create order out of chaos, to promote creativity over destruction, and to advocate peace. Above all, this hope challenges us to reach out with compassion, generosity, and forgiveness to what alone is of everlasting value in the community, the human person.

We are all hopers. And the Eucharist sends us forth to love and serve one another. I conclude with this. All Christian hope will be realized when the living Christ, by the power or fire of the Spirit, hands over the universe at the end-time to his heavenly Father.

BIBLIOGRAPHY

Augustine, Saint. *The Confessions of Saint Augustine*. Second ed. New York: Image Books, 1960.

Benedict of Nursia, Saint. *Rule of Life*. Circa 550.

Bennett, William J. *The Book of Virtues*. New York: Simon & Schuster, 1996.

Brooks, David. *The Road to Character*. New York: Random House, 2015.

Buechner, Frederick. *Whistling in the Dark*. New York: HarperOne, 1993.

Carlson, Richard. *Don't Sweat the Small Stuff: And It's All Small Stuff*. New York: Hachette Books, 1997.

Marcus, Steve. "Color Yogi a Happy Guy." *Newsday*, New York, February 24, 1986.

Dietrich, Jeff. *Broken and Shared*. Los Angeles: Marymount Institute Press/Tsehai Publishers, 2011.

Edelman, Marian Wright. *Lanterns: A Memoir of Mentors*. New York: Beacon Press, 1999.

Eliot, T. S. *Murder in the Cathedral*. 1935.

Francis of Assisi—The Saint: Early Documents. Vol. 1. Hyde Park, N.Y.: New City Press, 1999.

Friedman, Thomas. *The World Is Flat: A Brief History of the 21ˢᵗ Century*. New York: Farrar, Straus and Giroux, 2005.

Gawande, Atul. *Being Mortal: Medicine and What Matters in the End*. New York: Metropolitan Books, 2014.

Gumbel, Nicky. *The Jesus Lifestyle*. Revised ed. Alpha Books, 2007.

Guthrie, Suzanne. *Grace's Window: Entering the Season of Prayer*. New York: Morehouse Publishing, 2008.

Ignatius of Loyola, Saint. *The Spiritual Exercises of St. Ignatius*. Written 1522–24. Charlotte, N.C.: Tan Classics, 1999.

Keith, Kent. *Anyway: The Paradoxical Commandments*. New York: Berkley, 2003.

Keller, Helen. *The Story of My Life*. New ed. New York: Penguin, 1996.

King, Martin Luther, Jr. *A Gift of Love: Sermons from Strength to Love and other Preachings*. Boston: Beacon Press, 1963.

Kushner, Harold S. *Nine Essential Things I've Learned about Life*. Reprinted ed. Norwell, Mass.: Anchor, 2016.

Lawrence, T.E. *The Seven Pillars of Wisdom*. Hertfordshire, U.K.: Wordsworth Editions Ltd. 1926.

Lewis, C. S. *A Grief Observed*. New York: HarperOne, 2001.

Lewis, C. S. *The Problem of Pain*. Revised ed. New York: HarperOne, 2015.

McRaven, William. *Make Your Bed: Little Things That Can Change Your Life ... and Maybe the World*. New York: Grand Central Publishing, 2017.

Merton, Thomas. *The Seven Storey Mountain*. New York: Mariner Books, 1999.

Merton, Thomas. Prayer from *Thoughts in Solitude*. Farrar, Straus and Giroux, 1999.

Moody, Raymond A. *Life After Life*. MBB, Inc., 1975.

Newman, Blessed John Henry. "The Pillar of the Cloud" (Hymn: "Lead Kindly Light"), 1833.

Newman, Blessed John Henry. *An Essay on the Development of Christian Doctrine*. Composed 1845. Longmans, Green, and Co., London, 1909.

Niebuhr, Reinhold. "Serenity Prayer." 1943.

O'Neill, Eugene. *Lazarus Laughed: A Play for Imaginative Theatre*. 1925.

Peck, M. Scott. *The Road Less Traveled*. Anniversary ed. New York: Touchstone, 2003.

Smith, Emily Esfahani. *The Power of Meaning*. New York: Crown, 2017.

Ten Boom, Corrie. *The Hiding Place*. New York: Bantam Books, 1974.

Teresa of Avila, Saint. *Interior Castle*. 1577. New York: Image Books, 1961.

Therese of Lisieux, Saint. *The Story of a Soul*. 3rd ed. Washington, D.C.: ICS Publications, 1996.

Thomas of Aquinas, Saint. *Summa Theologiae*. Benziger Bros., 1947

Tolstoy, Leo. *A Confession and Other Religious Writings.* Reprint ed. New York: Penguin Classics, 1988.

Tolstoy, Leo. *The Death of Ivan Ilyich.* New York: Bantam Dell, 1981.

Wilder, Thornton. *Our Town: A Play in 3 Acts.* New York: Harper Perennial Modern Classics, 2003.

Yeats, William Butler. "The Second Coming." *Collected Poems of W. B. Yeats.* New York: Scribner, 1996.

Babette's Feast. DVD. Directed by Gabriel Axel, from a story by Isak Dinesen. Denmark: Just Betzer/MGM, 1987.

Printed in the United States
By Bookmasters